The Rwanda Genocide

DISCARD

Christina Fisanick, *Book Editor*

GAL

San Diego • Detroit • New York • San Francisco • Cleveland
New Haven, Conn. • Waterville, Maine • London • Munich

THOMSON

GALE

For more information, contact
Greenhaven Press
27500 Drake Rd.
Farmington Hills, MI 48331-3535
Or you can visit our Internet site at http://www.gale.com

Cover credit: © Adrian Arbib/CORBIS
UN Photo, 62
UN Photo 146504/Peter Magubane, 72

LIBRARY OF CONGRESS CATALOGING-IN-PUBLICATION DATA

Rwanda genocide / Christina Fisanick, book editor.
    p. cm. — (At issue in history)
Includes bibliographical references and index.
ISBN 0-7377-1985-0 (lib. : alk. paper) — ISBN 0-7377-1986-9 (pbk. : alk. paper)
    1. Genocide—Rwanda—History—20th century. 2. Rwanda—Ethnic relations—History—20th century. 3. Rwanda—History—Civil War, 1994—Atrocities. 4. Tutsi (African people)—Crimes against—Rwanda—History—20th century. 5. Hutu (African people)—Rwanda—Politics and government—20th century. I. Fisanick, Christina. II. Series.
DT450.435.R839 2004
967.57104'31—dc21   2003062479

Printed in the United States of America

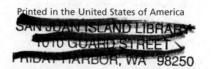

Contents

Chapter 1: The Causes of the Rwanda Genocide

Chapter 2: The International Community Failed to Respond

Chapter 3: Rebuilding Rwanda

Foreword

Historian Robert Weiss defines history simply as "a record and interpretation of past events." Both elements—record and interpretation—are necessary, Weiss argues.

> Names, dates, places, and events are the essence of history. But historical writing is not a compendium of facts. It consists of facts placed in a sequence to tell a connected story. A work of history is not merely a story, however. It also must analyze what happened and *why*—that is, it must interpret the past for the reader.

For example, the events of December 7, 1941, that led President Franklin D. Roosevelt to call it "a date which will live in infamy" are fairly well known and straightforward. A force of Japanese planes and submarines launched a torpedo and bombing attack on American military targets in Pearl Harbor, Hawaii. The surprise assault sank five battleships, disabled or sank fourteen additional ships, and left almost twenty-four hundred American soldiers and sailors dead. On the following day, the United States formally entered World War II when Congress declared war on Japan.

These facts and consequences were almost immediately communicated to the American people who heard reports about Pearl Harbor and President Roosevelt's response on the radio. All realized that this was an important and pivotal event in American and world history. Yet the news from Pearl Harbor raised many unanswered questions. Why did Japan decide to launch such an offensive? Why were the attackers so successful in catching America by surprise? What did the attack reveal about the two nations, their people, and their leadership? What were its causes, and what were its effects? Political leaders, academic historians, and students look to learn the basic facts of historical events and to read the intepretations of these events by many different sources, both primary and secondary, in order to develop a more complete picture of the event in a historical context.

In the case of Pearl Harbor, several important questions surrounding the event remain in dispute, most notably the role of President Roosevelt. Some historians have blamed his policies for deliberately provoking Japan to attack in order to propel America into World War II; a few have gone so far as to accuse him of knowing of the impending attack but not informing others. Other historians, examining the same event, have exonerated the president of such charges, arguing that the historical evidence does not support such a theory.

The Greenhaven At Issue in History series recognizes that many important historical events have been interpreted differently and in some cases remain shrouded in controversy. Each volume features a collection of articles that focus on a topic that has sparked controversy among eyewitnesses, contemporary observers, and historians. An introductory essay sets the stage for each topic by presenting background and context. Several chapters then examine different facets of the subject at hand with readings chosen for their diversity of opinion. Each selection is preceded by a summary of the author's main points and conclusions. A bibliography is included for those students interested in pursuing further research. An annotated table of contents and thorough index help readers to quickly locate material of interest. Taken together, the contents of each of the volumes in the Greenhaven At Issue in History series will help students become more discriminating and thoughtful readers of history.

Introduction

In one hundred days beginning in the spring of 1994, more than eight hundred thousand Rwandans were murdered. Bodies piled up in the streets, in abandoned schools, and in partially destroyed homes. The slaughter, which began on April 7, was not the result of a nuclear blast or the rampant spread of a contagious disease; rather, the people were killed by other citizens, neighbor against neighbor. Members of one Rwandan ethnic group, the Hutus, were killing members of another Rwandan ethnic group, the Tutsis, as well as other Tutsi-supporting Hutus. At first it was difficult for the rest of the world to understand what was taking place in this tiny African nation. Its history of recurrent civil wars cautioned other nations from intervening. Soon, however, as television coverage and eyewitness testimony revealed that these were premeditated, organized murders, the international community began to take notice. As the murders continued, often at a rate of a thousand or more a day, debates raged in the United States, France, the United Nations, and elsewhere around the globe over how to respond to what by the beginning of May certainly appeared different from prior Rwandan civil wars.

In the end, no foreign country intervened. The killings finally stopped only after the Rwandan Patriotic Army, a militant group primarily composed of Rwandan refugees, reclaimed Kigali, the capital city of Rwanda. Why did the United States, the United Nations, France, and other Western countries and organizations allow these bloody acts to continue? The answer to this question is complex and raises more questions. What did the world know, and when did the world know it? What are the presuppositions outsiders held and still hold about Africa and its people, and how did these affect their decisions during the genocide? What were the legal and ethical issues that impacted the decision to not assist the Rwandans during this time? As it would happen, the world's response to those events and the calamity that followed focused on the definition of a single term: *genocide.*

Before the Genocide

Rwanda, a landlocked, central African country slightly smaller than the state of Maryland, has had a long history of political, racial, and economic turmoil. Since its days of German and Belgian colonial rule in the late nineteenth century, Rwanda's government has been in constant flux. Finally gaining independence in 1962, Rwanda slowly began to establish a stable government.

The population of Rwanda is often described as being divided into two main groups: Tutsis and Hutus. Although there are some physical distinctions between the two groups (Hutus typically have darker skin than Tutsis), most scholars argue that it was the European colonists who exaggerated the differences between the groups and created animosity between them in order to gain political advantages. First the Germans and then the Belgians favored the Tutsi group by giving them superior roles in government and access to education that were denied to the Hutus. By the time of Rwandan independence in 1962, the Tutsis and the Hutus had become enemies fighting for political and social power.

After independence, foreign governments, such as France, Egypt, and the United States, continued to influence Rwanda's politics and economic system. At times, these foreign governments, as well as nongovernmental organizations, would favor one or the other ethnic group, furthering the divide between them. Civil wars became a regular part of Rwandan life. For example, on October 1, 1990, Rwandan exiles formed the Rwandan Patriotic Front (RPF) and invaded Rwanda from their base in Uganda. The RPF, composed primarily of Tutsis, blamed the Rwandan government for failing to address the problems of more than five hundred thousand Tutsi refugees living around the world. The war continued for almost two years until a cease-fire accord was signed on July 12, 1992, in Arusha, Tanzania.

The Genocide Cable

On January 11, 1994, Major General Roméo Dallaire, UN force commander in Rwanda, sent a cable to the UN headquarters in New York warning that mass killings were being planned. Dallaire urgently requested permission to act to prevent these killings and to protect the informant who told him, among other things, that he had trained seventeen hundred mostly Hutu rebels in military camps outside the capital. The informant, who was in charge of training the Hutu militia Interhamwe, told Dallaire that "in 20 minutes [my] personnel could kill up to 1000 Tutsis."[1] Despite the apparent credibility of this information, Kofi Annan, then head of UN peacekeeping, gave Dallaire the following instructions:

> Inform the President [of Rwanda] that you have received apparently reliable information concerning the activities of the Interhamwe militia which represents a clear threat to the peace process. You should inform him that these activities include the training and deployment of subversive groups in Kigali as well as the storage and distribution of weapons to these groups.[2]

In retrospect, this was a foolish order because President Juvenal Habyarimana was a Hutu and was partially responsible for creating these Hutu rebel forces.

In a 1999 interview with PBS *Frontline*, Iqbal Riza, chief of staff to Annan, stated that the United Nations could not have intervened in the way that Dallaire had requested because it was not in the organization's mandate, which was to maintain peace in Rwanda without using aggressive force. He asserted that no one saw the situation that Dallaire described as possible genocide but, rather, as a "political deadlock." Furthermore, given Rwanda's history of civil war, the UN assumed that this was another such situation. According to Riza:

> Since the 1960s, there have been cycles of violence— Tutsis against Hutus, Hutus against Tutsis. I'm sorry to put it so cynically. It was nothing new. This had continued from the '60s through the '70s into the '80s and here it was in the '90s.[3]

The Killings Begin

Just three months after these cables were exchanged, the genocide began. On April 6, 1994, a plane carrying Rwandan president Habyarimana and Burundian president Cyprien Ntaryamira was shot down just outside Kigali. Many commentators have speculated that Hutu extremists were responsible for the attack. According to experts, these extremists were angry because Habyarimana and Ntaryamira had just come from signing a peace accord in Arusha, Tanzania, in an attempt to end the discord between Hutus and Tutsis in Rwanda and Burundi. By doing so, Habyarimana was agreeing to stop funding the rebels and to place more Tutsis in government positions. The Hutu mob created and armed by Habyarimana deny any involvement in the plane crash. Nonetheless, his death sparked the genocide, which began at daybreak the following day.

The killings began early in the morning on April 7 and quickly spread throughout the country. Horrifying images of mutilated bodies in bombed-out churches appeared in international newspapers and on television news reports. By the end of the next day, U.S. president Bill Clinton had become aware of the events unfolding in Rwanda and issued a statement that expressed his shock and sadness. He also issued a statement to console the families of Americans who were in Rwanda and to let them know that the U.S. government was doing everything it could to ensure their safety. By April 9, the International Red Cross had estimated that tens of thousands of Rwandans had been murdered.

On April 24, following the murder of ten Belgian soldiers by Hutu rebels, the UN Security Council voted unanimously to withdraw most of the UNAMIR (United Nations Assistance Mission in Rwanda) troops, reducing the total force from 2,500 to 270. France and Belgium had already removed their armed forces, and the United States had evacuated its citizens. The Rwandan people were left with a skeletal force of UN troops to protect them from the daily slaughter that was going on in every neighborhood across their country.

On April 28, a reporter asked U.S. State Department spokeswoman Christine Shelley if what was happening in Rwanda was genocide. She responded that she did not consider it genocide and that "the use of the term 'genocide' has a very precise legal meaning, although it's not strictly a legal determination. There are other factors in there as well."[4] Critics contend that by this time the U.S. government knew that the events were genocide but were reluctant to label it as such. According to *Atlantic Monthly* reporter Samantha Power, "Whatever the inevitable imperfections of U.S. intelligence early on, the reports from Rwanda were severe enough to distinguish Hutu killers from ordinary combatants in civil war."[5] In other words, it should have been clear within the first two weeks of killing that what was occurring was genocide, even though U.S. officials waited until June 10 to label it as such.

Defining Genocide

Why was it so difficult to name these events in Rwanda? First, it is important to understand what the word *genocide* means. The Latin roots of *genocide* mean "tribal killing" (*genos* means tribe; *cide* means killing). Jurist Raphael Lemkin coined the term in 1933, but it did not become widely used until 1944, after the Jewish Holocaust. In his monograph *Axis Rule in Occupied Europe*, Lemkin defines genocide as the "practice of extermination of nations and ethnic groups."[6]

Four years later, in 1948, Lemkin's word was adopted by the United Nations, which created the "Convention on the Punishment and Prevention of the Crime of Genocide," also known as the Genocide Convention. In the declaration made at the convention and signed by members of the United Nations, genocide is described as "a crime under international law, contrary to the spirit and aims of the United Nations and condemned by the civilized world." The declaration then defines genocide very specifically:

> In the present Convention, genocide means any of the following acts committed with intent to destroy, in whole or in part, a national, ethnical, racial or religious group, as such: (a) Killing members of the group; (b) Causing serious bodily or mental harm to members of the group; (c) Deliberately inflicting on the group conditions of life calculated to bring about its physical destruction in whole or in part; (d) Imposing measures intended to prevent births within the group; (e) Forcibly transferring children of the group to another group.[7]

It has become obvious to most observers that the Rwanda killings were not random acts of violence but premeditated, willful acts of genocide. In a conference paper titled "Did or Did Not Genocide Take Place in Rwanda?" Carina Tertsakian of Amnesty International states that the events in Rwanda were clearly acts of genocide:

> There have been many cases documented where people were killed simply for being Tutsi or because they were thought to be Tutsi, whereas in fact maybe they weren't, and other cases of people being spared because they were known to be Hutu or thought to be Hutu.[8]

The Implications of the Term *Genocide*

Why should it matter what the violent acts were called when thousands of people were massacred by their friends and neighbors? According to the Genocide Convention, all member nations who signed the convention "confirm that genocide, whether committed in time of peace or in time of war, is a crime under international law which they undertake to prevent and to punish."[9] If the United Nations, the United States, and other Western nations had admitted at the time that the killings were in fact genocide, then they would have had to commit money and troops to stop them. For this reason, official representatives were extremely careful in using the term. *Genocide* is not simply a label but a legal term with legal consequences.

In a speech delivered at the Kigali airport on March 25, 1998, President Clinton apologized to the survivors of the genocide and their families. He stated that "we did not act quickly enough after the killing began" and that "we did not immediately call these crimes by their rightful name: genocide." Of course, by 1998, it was far too late to do anything but express regret and, as Clinton stated, to encourage the world to "work together as a community of civilized nations to strengthen our ability to prevent and, if necessary, to stop genocide."[10]

Would It Have Made a Difference?

At this point, more than ten years after the bloody events in Rwanda came to an end, very few people are still questioning whether the world knew what was happening was genocide or not. Fewer still argue that it was not genocide. Yet some people still wonder if it would have made a difference had the world acknowledged that these events were genocide and acted according to the laws of the Genocide Convention.

There seems to be little question that had the United Nations responded to Dallaire's cable and given him the power to take action, then the genocide could most probably have been prevented. At the very least, if the total number of UNAMIR troops had not been cut or had been increased, more lives could have been saved. However, even though the United Nations and some Western countries are willing to acknowledge their failure to stop the Rwandan genocide, most world leaders are quick to point out that the Rwandans who did the killing should bear the greatest burden of the blame. Iqbal Riza makes this point quite clearly:

> With all due respect, those who were responsible for the loss of lives were those who had planned the killing. They are responsible for the loss of life. We did not anticipate that this was going to happen. Yes, we made a mistake. We deeply regret it. We failed there.[11]

Some have argued that it is simply not the role of the United States or any other government's role to intervene every time war and killing erupt in a country. Nonetheless, as political writer Stephen J. Pope has pointed out, "A realistic sense of [America's] limited power does not make it legitimate for us to turn our backs on the massive numbers of innocent people who were slaughtered."[12] Unfortunately, it is too late to save the lives of the thousands of Rwandans who were killed during the genocide. However, the world can act together not only to ensure that the perpetrators of these atrocious crimes are punished but also to prevent such crimes from happening again.

Soon after the end of the genocide, the International Criminal Tribunal for Rwanda (ICTR) was created to bring the criminals to justice. The transcripts of these trials will serve as an unbiased history of the Rwanda genocide in the hopes that it will not be forgotten or repeated. As with those of the Nuremberg trials that followed the Holocaust, the records of these trials should preserve the history. According to the Center for International Human Rights:

> The more ringleaders indicted, based on evidence publicly detailed by the prosecutor, the more the factual record of Rwanda's genocide will be credibly preserved for history. Future revisionists may deny it, even as crackpot academics and Neo-Nazis now deny the Holocaust, but the indictments will stand against them.[13]

Notes

1. Quoted in Kofi Annan, "Cable from Kofi Annan to Roméo Dallaire," January 11, 1994, on *Frontline: The Triumph of Evil*, January 1999. www.pbs.org.
2. Annan, "Cable from Kofi Annan to Roméo Dallaire."
3. "Interview with Iqbal Riza," on *Frontline: The Triumph of Evil*, January 1999. www.pbs.org.

4. Quoted in "Interview with Iqbal Riza."
5. Samantha Power, "Bystanders to Genocide: Why the United States Let the Rwandan Tragedy Happen," *Atlantic Monthly*, September 11, 2001. www.theatlantic.com.
6. Quoted in S.D. Stein, "Genocide: Definitions and Controversies," *Web Genocide Documentation Centre: Resources on Genocide, War Crimes, and Mass Killing*, June 24, 2002. www.ess.uwe.ac.uk.
7. United Nations, "Convention on the Punishment and Prevention of the Crime of Genocide," *Web Genocide Documentation Centre: Resources on Genocide, War Crimes, and Mass Killing*, December 9, 1948. www.ess.uwe.ac.uk.
8. Carina Tertsakian, "Did or Did Not Genocide Take Place in Rwanda?" Africa Direct Conference, London, July 27, 1998. www.udayton.edu.
9. United Nations, "Convention on the Punishment and Prevention of the Crime of Genocide."
10. Bill Clinton, "Speech at Kigali, Rwanda Airport," reported by the Associated Press, March 25, 1998.
11. "Interview with Iqbal Riza."
12. Stephen J. Pope, "The Politics of Apology and the Slaughter in Rwanda," *America*, March 6, 1999, p. 9.
13. Center for International Human Rights, "Rwanda: A Little Justice at Last, Maybe," *World View Commentary*, February 21, 1996.

Chapter **1**

The Causes of the Rwanda Genocide

1

President Habyarimana's Government Was Responsible for the Genocide

Fergal Keane

British Broadcasting Corporation (BBC) journalist Fergal Keane was reporting on the upcoming multiracial elections in South Africa in April 1994 when the Rwanda genocide began. From his home in Johannesburg, South Africa, Keane saw the first broadcast images of the massive slaughter and eventually traveled with a camera and sound crew to report on the events taking place in war-torn Rwanda. Along the way, he kept diary notes and photographs of what he saw. He is still haunted by the horrific memories of that time, which he discusses in his book *Season of Blood: A Rwandan Journey*. In the prologue, an excerpt from which is included here, he discusses his perspective on the causes behind the genocide. He disagrees with the argument that the genocide was the result of long-held tribal hatred between the two predominant ethnic groups, the Hutu and Tutsi. Keane argues instead that Rwanda's president Juvénal Habyarimana and his government created and dispersed the hate propaganda that encouraged the Hutu people to rise up against their Tutsi friends and neighbors. Keane also asserts that French intervention and economic problems contributed to the outbreak of mass killings that ultimately took place.

Fergal Keane, *Season of Blood: A Rwandan Journey*. New York: Viking, 1995. Copyright © 1995 by Fergal Keane. All rights reserved. Reproduced by permission of Viking, a division of Penguin Putnam Inc.

17

When the genocide started on the night of 6 April 1994, I was sitting at home in Johannesburg preparing for the multi-racial elections in South Africa. To be frank I paid only scant attention to the news reports emerging from Kigali. I have vague recollections of news bulletins describing how the aircraft carrying Juvénal Habyarimana, the president of Rwanda, and Cyprien Ntaryamira, the president of Burundi, had crashed in the grounds of the presidential palace in Kigali [the capital of Rwanda]. In the days that followed there came a succession of stories about massacres across Rwanda. I was too preoccupied with the dramatic events unfolding in South Africa to give the matter anything more than cursory attention. Colleagues from London and Nairobi were being dispatched to Rwanda, and there didn't seem much point in my becoming sidetracked. The world's attention was focused on the elections and, having spent four years preparing for that moment, I was in no mood to head for Rwanda. In the second week of April film began to arrive in Johannesburg for transmission to British and American television networks. Much of the material seemed to be coming from the border between Rwanda and Tanzania, the Rusomo Falls Bridge, across which tens of thousands of refugees were pouring each day. There were some fearful pictures coming out of Kigali: mounds of bodies and roadblocks manned by machete-wielding gangs. The general consensus among those of us watching the pictures and those who had taken them was that Rwanda was a madhouse, a primitive torture chamber where rival tribes were busy settling ancient scores. I could not, watching the apocalyptic images unfolding on the video screens, imagine Rwanda as a country in its own right—a place with cities and schools and universities, with a wide diversity of media and political organizations, a country with musicians and poets. The idea that the madness might have been planned, that it was the direct result of political scheming, was far from my thoughts. I knew only that large-scale violence had been a feature of Rwandan life since independence [from Belgium on July 1, 1962]. Both Rwanda and its neighbour Burundi had seen frequent massacres of one ethnic group or another. To most in the international community the words 'Tutsi' and 'Hutu' [the names of the two main ethnic groups in Rwanda] were synonymous with tribal slaughter.

Media Perceptions of Rwanda

The mass of early reporting of the Rwandan killings conveyed the sense that the genocide was the result of some innate inter-ethnic loathing that had erupted into irrational violence. This probably had a lot to do with the fact that major news organizations visited Rwanda and neighbouring Burundi only when there was major violence: in for a week or two to cover the slaughter and then back out again. A friend of mine, Sam Kiley of the London *Times*, rightly describes this as the 'kids in the fridge school of journalism'—in other words, a journalism driven by stories of horror but markedly lacking in analysis or historical context.

The coverage of violence in Central Africa, beginning with the horrors of the Congo in the sixties and seventies, has followed a predictable pattern. As soon as news of the killings begins to spread, the cameras arrive and the focus of attention is almost universally on the body count and the plight of the survivors. If there are Europeans to be rescued they are invariably the main news priority. The political, social and psychological factors that play a part in shaping the madness are given little analysis.

Where television is concerned, African news is generally only big news when it involves lots of dead bodies.

Much of the coverage of Rwanda in the early days neglected the part that power and money had played in the calculations of those who launched the genocide. Where television is concerned, African news is generally only big news when it involves lots of dead bodies. The higher the mound, the greater the possibility that the world will, however briefly, send its camera teams and correspondents. Once the story has gone 'stale', i.e. there are no new bodies and the refugees are down to a trickle, the circus moves on. The powerful images leave us momentarily horrified but largely ignorant, what somebody memorably described as having 'compassion without understanding'. Thus a well-planned campaign of politically and materially motivated slaughter can come to be explained away as an ancient tribal conflict because the men and women on the ground have been moved on before there is time to investigate properly. This is more true of television than of any other media, but several of the world's leading newspapers also bought the line, in the initial stages, that the killings were a straightforward 'tribal war'.

Not Just Tribal Hatred

Rwanda's genocide was not a simple matter of mutual hatred between tribes erupting into irrational violence. Neither were the mass killings the result of a huge and sudden outpouring of rage on the part of Hutus following the murder of their president. The killings—and there is ample documentary evidence to prove this—were planned long in advance by a clique close to President Habyarimana himself. This clique—which included members of the president's immediate family and his in-laws—bitterly resented the prospect of power-sharing with the Tutsi minority. Any democratization of Rwanda's effective one-party state would have had disastrous consequences for the clique, who had powerful backers in the army and who had created their own civilian militia—the Interahamwe—to prepare for the day of vengeance against those who would seek a share of power. For several years prior to the genocide Hutus were exposed to an ongoing and virulent campaign of anti-Tutsi brainwashing. The report of the human rights group African Rights (*Death, Despair and Defiance*) provides a comprehensive and damning account of this process of brainwashing and is recommended reading for anyone who doubts that the genocide was well planned.

The average citizen had a subsistence existence.

The ostensible targets of the hatred were the rebels of the Rwandan Patriotic Front (RPF) [a group of Rwandan refugees], who had launched an invasion of the country from neighbouring Uganda in October 1990. But the subtext of the numerous public condemnations of the RPF was clear enough: no Tutsi was to be trusted. All were members of a fifth column planning to reimpose a Tutsi autocracy on Rwanda. To peasants with a long folk memory of past Tutsi misrule, the warnings and the increasingly hysterical propaganda had a powerful effect. Tens of thousands became in-

fected—and I can think of no other word that can describe
the condition—by an anti-Tutsi psychosis; they were convinced through newspapers, radio and the frequent public
speeches of Habyarimana's closest supporters that the Tutsis
were going to turn them into beasts of the field once again.

The Hutu extremists, most of them members or supporters of the ruling party, produced a set of Ten Commandments that dictated how Hutus should treat their Tutsi
neighbours. Among other things it described as 'traitors' any
Hutu who married, befriended or employed Tutsis; all Tutsis were dishonest and they were to be excluded from business and from positions of influence in education; crucially
the Commandments—given wide circulation in Rwanda—
urged Hutus to 'stop having mercy on the Batutsi'. This last
injunction was to be obeyed by thousands of Hutu peasants
when the genocide began. The theology of hate espoused by
the extremists was remarkably similar to that of the Nazis in
their campaign against the Jews prior to the outbreak of the
Second World War. It was designed to marginalize the Tutsis and create an atmosphere in which their mass destruction
would be acceptable, almost inevitable.

Radio Mille Collines

The role of the privately owned [Rwandan] radio station
Radio Mille Collines has been widely mentioned in reporting of the Rwandan genocide. Controlled by Hutu extremists with close links to Habyarimana's family, it was also fi-
nancially supported by the president. On 6 April, the day of
the plane crash, Radio Mille Collines told its audience that
'Tutsis needed to be killed'. The theme was to dominate the
station's broadcasts for weeks. The official state radio was
only marginally less virulent, constantly calling on the
Hutus to rise up and defend Rwanda against the invasion of
the *inyenzi*, or 'cockroaches'. Several privately owned newspapers and journals were harnessed for the task of dissemi-
nating hate propaganda. As far as the training of the militia
is concerned, there is abundant evidence implicating senior
government ministers and government officials with responsibility for its genocidal agenda. Foreign diplomats, a
few visiting journalists and human rights experts had been
warning for several months about the training of large
groups of armed Hutu extremists. Given the kind of hatred
being spewed out on radio and in the newspapers, nobody

could have doubted what the militia was being prepared for. The United Nations, African Rights and the new Rwandan government have prepared lists of ministers and army officers and local officials for the purpose of war crimes trials. Nearly all had been active in promoting Hutu nationalism and obsessive anti-Tutsi propaganda long before the genocide actually occurred. At its most obvious this could take the form of simple murder—attacks on isolated Tutsi communities as practice runs for the final solution. More often than not, it simply involved spreading the word of hatred far and wide. . . .

Refugees Flee to Uganda

Many of the Rwandan Tutsis who became refugees in 1959 and 1962 [during Hutu rebellions] fled to [nearby] Uganda, settling in the south and centre of the country. There as many as 200,000 people attempted to create new lives in a country that itself was experiencing a traumatic evolution into nationhood. They left with bitter memories and a burning desire to one day come back. Their country of exile was to suffer the terror of rule by Milton Obote (twice) and Idi Amin. A substantial proportion of the Tutsi refugees settled in the Luwero triangle, an area singled out for particularly cruel treatment by both Amin's and Obote's forces. The experience of terror at the hands of the Ugandan army convinced the refugees that their only future lay within Rwanda. Many of their children joined the National Resistance Army of Yoweri Museveni, which eventually overthrew the government of Obote in 1986. Museveni's army had a reputation for discipline and military professionalism, and many of the senior commanders were Rwandan Tutsis. These 'children of '59' regrouped after the end of the Ugandan war and formed into the RPF, determined to return to the country of their forefathers.

Eradicating the Tutsis

In their absence Rwanda followed the well-trodden, post-independence path to a corrupt one-party state. The average citizen had a subsistence existence. The PARME-HUTU [The Party for the Emancipation of the Hutus] elite siphoned off vast sums in public funds and turned the civil service into a party jobs machine. Clientelism thrived, and discrimination against Tutsis was widespread and systematic. There were occasional violent pogroms [organized massacres] throughout the sixties, which was a period of fear and uncertainty in Rwanda. Attacks by bands of Tutsi guerrillas (nicknamed *inyenzi*, or 'cockroaches', by the government) led to vicious reprisals. In one such pogrom in 1963 Hutu militias murdered an estimated 10,000 Tutsis.

Hutu extremism was essentially a useful tool by which the corrupt elite that ran the country could hold on to power.

There was a further outbreak in 1967—again the Tutsis were butchered and dumped in the rivers—and then a large-scale purge of Tutsis from the universities in 1973. This expanded into a wider pogrom designed to drive the minority from all of the country's educational institutions. As violence spread throughout the country the army's chief of staff, Juvénal Habyarimana, stepped in and staged a *coup d'état* under the pretext of restoring order. Instigating violence and then staging a *coup* in order to quell the same violence is a favoured tactic among potential dictators. It is widely suspected that Habyarimana was behind the 1973 disturbances. Whatever his motives, Habyarimana's rule did not, as many Tutsis had feared, precipitate a total onslaught against the minority. On the contrary, Habyarimana appeared to go out of his way to stress national unity and appealed for an end to ethnic bloodletting. But behind the scenes Habyarimana simply swopped the old southern and central power elite of the PARMEHUTU for his own northern cronies. The northern Hutus . . . were the most fierce ethnic chauvinists in Rwanda. This had much to do with their experience at the hands of the Germans and their Tutsi allies, who subdued the north in the early part of the century. In power Habyarimana may not have murdered the Tutsis with the same fervour as his predecessors but he was relentless in the task of discrimination and scapegoating. While he and his family and friends filled foreign bank accounts with the country's wealth, the position of the Rwandan peasantry went from bad to worse. Vast sums of aid sent by foreign governments and agencies went either directly or indirectly into the pockets of senior government ministers and officials. Habyarimana's party, the National Revolutionary

Movement for Development (Mouvement Révolutionnaire National pour le Développement, or MRND), dedicated itself to the enrichment of the northern Hutu elite while the peasants were encouraged to blame the Tutsis for their problems. Again there are echoes of the Nazis' scapegoating of the Jews in the thirties. While the president and his cronies grew fat the economic situation steadily worsened. Rwanda is one of the smallest countries in the world, with a land area of just over 26,000 kilometres. The population density is the highest in Africa. As many as 400 people are in theory dependent on each square kilometre of land. But this has not prevented Rwandans from being able to feed themselves throughout most of the country's years of independence. A heavy population density does not necessarily translate into the kind of famine witnessed in countries like Sudan and Ethiopia. Rwanda has rich soil and a plentiful supply of rainfall. When famine or severe hunger has taken place it has been largely due to factors such as war or external economic pressures. For example the coffee price (coffee accounted for 75 per cent of Rwanda's export earnings) collapsed in 1989 and led to severe hardship for hundreds of thousands of farmers. The ongoing war with the RPF since 1990 caused huge population movements, disturbing the fragile economic balance in the areas that had experienced the influx of refugees. The upheavals increased the competition for scarce resources and made the mass of Hutu peasants fearful for the security of their land. The extremists told them repeatedly that the Tutsis were coming to seize their land. In reality the thieving of resources was being done by Habyarimana and his cronies. But western donors increased pressure for some kind of economic and political accountability. Slowly but surely the wealth tap was shut off; the money and jobs that had been used to buy the loyalty of the military and the civil service were in danger of disappearing. The implications of any democratization of society were horrifying to the elite: without political power the whole system of patronage and clientelism would collapse.

RPF Offensive

When guerrillas of the Tutsi-dominated RPF staged their offensive in 1990 the Habyarimana regime seized the opportunity for a major and dangerous exercise in scapegoating. Aware of mounting discontent in the countryside, the president and the entire organizational machinery of the MRND and military began to actively foment fear and hatred of the Tutsis. By this stage Tutsis living within Rwanda were already heavily penalized: there were only two Tutsi members of parliament, only one Tutsi town mayor, no Tutsi regional mayors and only one Tutsi ambassador. There were almost no Tutsis in the army and the police. To even vaguely imply that they were still a privileged elite was plainly ludicrous. However, Habyarimana and his clique (known as the Akazu, or 'little hut') began to build up a civilian militia—the Interahamwe, or 'Those who stand together'—which, with the army and the presidential guard, would be used to protect MRND power and privilege. The theory behind the anti-Tutsi propaganda was simple: rather than lose power to a growing opposition movement led by Hutu moderates and including Tutsis, the MRND would drag the old bogey out of the closet and direct the anger of the poor in the direction of the Tutsis. This would provide the people with a pressure valve and remove, literally, any potent opposition to MRND rule. Privilege would be maintained albeit at the expense of fomenting ethnic hatred. It is not known whether Habyarimana intended the killing to reach the scale that it did after his death. What can be said is that he encouraged the most virulent anti-Tutsi propaganda and that, given Rwanda's history, he must have been aware of the potential consequences. There had also been a growing number of attacks on Tutsis inside Rwanda between 1989 and the actual start of the genocide in April 1994. Habyarimana did nothing to quell the violence that was being instigated by his henchmen in the militia and army. Hutu extremism was essentially a useful tool by which the corrupt elite that ran the country could hold on to power.

France Intervenes

Habyarimana might have been able to ride the tiger and survive had the weight of international pressure and the RPF's growing military strength not forced him to compromise. Having treated earlier ceasefire and democracy agreements with contempt, he was finally forced to concede the principle of multi-party politics in 1991. A number of political parties were formed, including the Democratic Republican Movement (Mouvement Démocratique Républicain, or MDR), whose members were singled out for particularly vicious treatment later on. The MDR represented a credible, Hutu-dominated opposition to Habyarimana. He responded by accusing opposition political groups of acting as the lackeys of the RPF, and he tacitly encouraged the setting up of the Hutu extremist Coalition for the Defence of the Republic—a breakaway of the ruling party that was in a position to propagate virulent anti-Tutsi policies at a publicly safe distance from Habyarimana. It is vital to remember that while publicly proclaiming himself willing to reform the president was privately financing and helping to organize the Hutu extremist militias. Any true democratization of Rwanda could conceivably have seen Habyarimana and his allies facing trial for their part in earlier purges against the Tutsis and their political opponents. In February 1993 an offensive by the RPF considerably weakened the president's negotiating position. The RPF moved towards Kigali and might have seized the city had French troops not intervened on the side of the government.

The murder of the president would provide the perfect pretext for implementing the final solution of the Tutsi problem.

The French had long supported Habyarimana and had no wish to see him driven from power by the rebels. The pro-Habyarimana faction in Paris was led by François Mitterrand's [president of France from 1981 until 1995] son Jean-Christophe [adviser on African affairs,], who saw Rwanda as part of a Francophone Africa under threat from the encroachments of the English-speaking nations to the north and east, i.e. Uganda and Tanzania. Among Jean-Christophe's gifts to the Rwandan president was the personal jet that was shot out of the sky on 6 April. The implication of this friendship was clear: if the price for maintaining some degree of French influence was the preservation of despots and kleptocrats, then Paris was always more than willing to pay. In contrast to Habyarimana the leaders of the RPF were largely English-speaking. The long years of exile in Uganda had forced the Tutsi refugees to abandon the French language. For their part the French maintained a military mission and a sizeable detachment of intelligence officers in Rwanda. With their contacts inside the army and at every level of government and the state media, Paris could not have been ignorant of the genocidal intentions of many of the senior officers and officials. For the French to suggest otherwise would be a lamentable comment on the abilities of their own intelligence services and diplomats.

Arusha Peace Accords

However, French assistance was not enough to save Habyarimana's regime from the combined effects of RPF military pressure and international agitation for democratization. By having seized the military initiative the RPF was ultimately able to force Habyarimana into negotiations that culminated in the Arusha Peace Accords of August 1993. The ten-day talks at Arusha in Tanzania produced a series of protocols, the most significant of which were those on power-sharing, a dramatic reduction in the powers of the presidency and, crucially, the integration of the RPF into the armed forces. The rebels were to provide 40 per cent of the troops for the army lower ranks and 50 per cent of the officer corps. Under huge international pressure Habyarimana put his signature to the accords. Although he still did everything in his power to split the opposition and maintain absolute power, the domestic and international pressure was too much. Almost every international representative who met him in the weeks leading up to his assassination sensed that Habyarimana was coming to terms—albeit unwillingly—with reality: either share power or face war with the RPF and international isolation.

Habyarimana's Death

The Arusha Peace Accords were to be his death warrant. The extremists he had cultivated and the men who had grown rich during the days of the one-party state were not about to see their privilege disappear with the stroke of a pen. Now, instead of holding fast, Habyarimana was weakening, threatening to pull the house down around them. It was time to install a more reliable man. On the evening of 6 April, as Habyarimana was returning from a session of negotiations at Arusha, two missiles were fired at his jet as it landed at Kigali International Airport. The most likely explanation—one disputed by Hutu extremists and their French supporters—is that soldiers of the presidential guard based next to the airport fired the missiles. There is another theory that members of the French military or security services, or mercenaries in the pay of France, shot down the aircraft. Although no firm proof has been produced, there are senior figures in the Belgian security services who think the French may have wanted rid of Habyarimana, believing he was about to hand the country over to the RPF. The jet crashed into the grounds of the presidential palace, which is close to the airport. Habyarimana was killed, along with the president of Burundi, Cyprien Ntaryamira and the chief of staff of Rwanda's army, Deogratias Nsabimana. The MRND government immediately blamed the RPF—and, by extension, all Tutsis—for the killing, suggesting that somehow RPF soldiers had managed to locate themselves next to the biggest army base in the country and murder the president. It was possible, of course, but highly improbable. The RPF had Habyarimana where it wanted him: weak and increasingly susceptible to pressure. On the other hand the army and the extremists had every reason to be rid of him: his death would create a political vacuum that would be filled by an interim government made up of Hutu extremists. Such a government would be in a position to disavow all agreements reached by its predecessor. The days of privilege would return. More importantly, the murder of the president would provide the perfect pretext for implementing the final solution of the Tutsi problem, as well as for the destruction of moderate Hutu opposition politicians. The army and the militias were ready with lists of their enemies; the extremist radio stations and newspapers had already created an atmosphere of anti-Tutsi hysteria. All that remained was for the signal to be given. No sooner had Habyarimana's jet been shot down than the killings began in earnest. The one hundred days of genocide had been launched.

2

Socioeconomic Conditions, Not Ethnic Hatred, Led to the Genocide

Villia Jefremovas

In 1984 Villia Jefremovas began studying the brick- and tile-making industries of Rwanda. As a professor of geography and environmental studies at Canada's Carleton University, she became interested in what in the mid-1980s was a thriving, productive country. All that changed ten years later with the genocide of more than eight hundred thousand Rwandans and the destruction of many of the very brickyards that she had studied. In 2002 she published a book detailing her study and reflecting on how these industries were impacted by the genocide. In her last chapter, a portion of which is included here, she takes up the argument of what caused the genocide in the first place. Unlike many scholars and policy makers who cite ethnic hatred as the motivating factor behind the hundred-day massacre, Jefremovas asserts that poverty, decreased land availability, population growth, regional politics, and a number of other seemingly unrelated socioeconomic issues were the real reasons violence erupted on April 8, 1994. She also argues that the desperate plight of the people made them more vulnerable to the propaganda and political manipulation of the Rwandan government, encouraging the Hutus to rise up against the Tutsis.

The media have emphasized the role of ethnicity and ethnic poltics in [the Rwandan genocide] and imbued them with an air of inevitability as one more example of "tribal violence" in Africa. A closer look shows that the factors that made the genocide possible are more complex and less inevitable than these reports would suggest. Economic recession, economic restructuring, population growth, patterns of elite access to power, regional politics, civil war, "democratization," the politics of other countries of the Great Lakes region, and international policies all played a role in the move to the genocide. This [selection] will examine the background to the genocide [and] consider the role that class and regional differences played in the spread of the genocide across the country. . . . The factors that conditioned the development of these small industries [the brickyards]—the centralization of power; the transformations in land tenure and access to resources; regional disparities; and the growth of self-interested elites; coupled with war, economic crisis, and structural adjustment, were also the factors that underlay the politics of the 1994 genocide. . . .

Background to the Genocide

From the mid-1980s on, the economic growth that Rwanda had experienced in the 1970s and early 1980s under the [Juvénal] Habyarimana regime slowed dramatically and by 1989, after the dramatic fall in coffee prices, Rwanda's principal export, the regime was faced with the need to restructure its economy. The same period saw growing corruption of functionaries and an increasing distance of these functionaries from the predominantly rural population. The main benefits of the state, access to land, power, education, and jobs, were concentrated into the hands of a smaller and smaller elite within the government, at a time during which population growth and ecological decline placed increasing pressure on these resources. The 1989 fall in coffee prices brought this economic crisis to a head. Coffee prices fell by 50% in 1989 and hundreds of thousands of households lost 50% of their cash income because coffee was a small holder crop. The economic restructuring that followed, through an IMF (International Monetary Fund) [an organization that monitors the global economy and provides loans to struggling nations] structural adjustment program caused food prices to soar, salaries to fall, public services to collapse, and led to a 40% devaluation of the Rwandan franc. Several areas of the country suffered a drought and, for the first time since independence [from Belgium in 1962], people could not afford to buy food, emergency stocks were reduced, and people died of hunger.

Amid this economic and political crisis the rich became much richer.

During this period, on October 1, 1990, the Rwandan Patriotic Front (RPF) [a militant group of Rwandan refugees] invaded Rwanda. The Rwandan army was totally unprepared and the RPF almost made it to Kigali [the capital of Rwanda]. They were beaten back only by the intervention of Rwandan, Belgian, and French troops. The government used this opportunity to jail its enemies, Tutsi and Hutu, and to increase political repression in the country. Economically, the war funneled most of the available resources and aid money into arms and expanding the army, which grew from 5,000 to 50,000 during the years that followed, and arms flooded the country.

At the same time, the population bomb exploded. There was little land for the new cohort of youth reaching the age of majority in an economy that remained based on agriculture and in which few nonfarm options existed or had been created. From the 1940s to the mid-1980s, new lands were opened up and this helped deal with the population pressure, but by the 1980s [according to sociologist Jennifer Olsen,] "these options were virtually exhausted." There was no new land to be opened up and farm sizes shrank to an average of 0.7 hectares. These young men had nothing to inherit and had few nonfarm options. Until the economic restructuring, Habyarimana's regime had provided a few rural-based projects to absorb some of these youth, but even these relatively ineffectual efforts disappeared with restructuring. Peasants also lost access to health care, schooling, and other services that had been subsidized by the state, while the elites took advantage of the new opportunities that restructuring presented.

Amid this economic and political crisis the rich became much richer. Prominent among the richest of the rich were the military, government officials, and the supporters of

Habyarimana, most of whom were drawn from the north of Rwanda. Every region saw the growth of an elite that had fewer and fewer connections with the peasantry, and increasingly this elite openly disparaged the rural and poor. Emergency land sales skyrocketed, and land concentration escalated. While 86% of the population lived below the poverty line, the income share of the wealthiest decile [tenth] of the population increased from 22% in 1982 to 52% in 1994. One informant summed up this transformation succinctly when he said, "We, the elites, were so comfortable in those last years, running after the new things we could have for the first time, that we forgot about the problems of the poor."

The late 1980s and early 1990s saw a heightening of political opposition and calls for democratization, as well as growing criticism in the international community of the Habyarimana regime. The world community responded to the criticism by pushing for democratization. However, this push did not lead to a real opening up of the political processes; rather it "facilitated an expansion of the elite class within the closed arena of national politics." [Sociologists] Catherine Newbury and David Newbury argue that "substantive democracy in any meaningful sense was not at issue," despite popular involvement in pushing for transition. Because of structural adjustment, even those elites interested in pushing for reforms had little control over the means to meet the expectations of the populace.

Political neglect and poverty played a powerful part in ensuring complicity with the genocide in Gikongoro.

The civil war also played an important role in this lack of resources. Most of the resources were funneled into the hands of the military and their hardcore allies within the government, the two groups most resistant to democracy. The transition government, put into place in 1992, did nothing to change the nature of political power in Rwanda, with new elites simply being co-opted by this system. However, it did lead to an increase in popular dissatisfaction and popular disaffection with the ruling elites. This led to a greater pillaging of the economy, greater debt, and more disparity while the war helped fuel the "ethnic" rhetoric of the extremist parties. The growth of these parties under international pressure and scrutiny also gave the opposition a false sense of security in an atmosphere of economic crisis and extremism. An informant commented bitterly, "All that multipartyism did was write the death lists." Like many political demagogues before them, Habyarimana, his regime, and other factions of the elite dealt with the unemployment crisis by arming this mass of disaffected youth. For a select group of youth, membership in the militias meant an income, power, and a place to belong.

> *Throughout the country the so-called spontaneous violence can be shown to have been systematic and cold-blooded.*

As discontent with the Habyarimana regime grew, so did the government propaganda, which stressed the fact that the Tutsi were the enemy and the ancient oppressors of Rwanda. The period between 1990 and 1994 saw the development of racist propaganda that made the genocide possible. The press, radio, and television propaganda featured the manipulation, simplification, and reduction of history, reducing ethnicity and politics of Rwanda to ethnic politics. [According to historian Jean-Pierre Chretien,] these media contributed to the evolution of a "logic of genocide" to rationalize the dictatorship of President Juvenal Habyarimana, and entrenched the power of a small segment of the elite associated with this regime. . . .

Anti-Tutsi sentiment could also be manipulated so successfully because of the precolonial and colonial history of Rwanda and the makeup of the Rwandan Patriotic Front [RPF] that was predominantly Tutsi. Some were drawn from the descendants of the aristocrats and their dependents who fled Rwanda from 1959 to 1963, and some were drawn from the commoners and aristocrats who fled the broader-based persecutions of 1963 onward. The regime fostered by the Belgians was very rapacious, very corrupt, and linked to a racist ideology that excluded the majority of Hutu from power, access to education, and the benefits of state clientage. The majority of the peasantry was terrified by the prospect of the return of this form of rule. The RPF did little to allay these fears. In their 1993 offensive, when they came within 40 kilometers of the capital, Kigali, they drove 700,000 predominantly Hutu peasants out of some of the most densely populated areas of the north and into Kigali and the south, in order to put pressure on the Habyarimana regime. This expulsion provided a propaganda coup for the Habyarimana regime and [according to Catherine Newbury and David Newbury] "undermined the efforts of RPF to present itself as a political movement committed to gaining the confidence of the population and interested in the welfare of the population." Even though there was no evidence that they had any intention of reinstating a "feudal state" as the anti-Tutsi propaganda incessantly stated, the RPF by its actions fed into the fears of the peasantry.

This fear, which had been fed by the racist propaganda of the regime during the 1990s in the journals, newspapers, and through the quasi-private radio and television station, Radio-Télévision Libre Milles Collines (RTLM), was intensified by events in Burundi [which led to several Hutu leaders and politicians being murdered in October 1993], despite the fact that the vast majority of the Tutsi in Rwanda were poor peasants living in equivalent circumstances as their neighbors. The Habyarimana regime responded to the various crises it faced and the civil war was a deliberate use of ethnic violence for political ends. The killings were ordered from above. They were state-sponsored and backed by a power group of the military. Although a horrendous number were carried out by civilians, the majority were carried out by the militias. However, this reality disguises the extent to which the genocide, depending on political leadership, local class relations, and local history, did not follow the same pattern throughout Rwanda.

The Patterns of Killing

When Habyarimana's airplane went down on April 6, 1994, [which was also carrying Burundian president Cyprein Ntaryamira and thought to have been shot down by members of Habyarimana's government] a number of things happened or did not happen: (1) most of the military stayed in its barracks waiting for the RPF; (2) the Presidential Guard and the Interahamwe (the Mouvement Révolutionaire pour le Développement [MRND]/CDR militias) [Hutu civilian extremists] went out to kill the opposition (the majority of whom were Hutu), the critics of the government (the majority of whom were Hutu), and Tutsi leaders; (3) other landless youth and the urban poor went rampaging through the wealthy Kigali neighborhoods; and (4) only some regions of Rwanda responded to the command to start killing. If we consider the development of the genocide throughout the country in the 1991–1993 period and in 1994, we will see that the violence was neither spontaneous nor the result of "ancient hatreds." The killings did not erupt throughout the whole country; instead, many regions stayed calm through weeks of bloodshed. The killings, where they took place, were orchestrated by various elites and targeted different groups with different degrees of success throughout the country. Each region and areas within each region either resisted or became involved for different reasons. The genocide was only the last of a series of attempts to incite ethnic violence in Rwanda but, as in the case of the Kayabanda regime in 1973 [under which Tutsis were purged from the universities], these first attempts met with limited success.

Looking at the pattern of killings in the period between 1991 and 1993, it can be seen that the major ethnic/political massacres and attacks were concentrated in Gisenyi, Ruhengeri, and Kibuye. In the genocide of 1994, we see a similar pattern. The killings in Gisenyi, Ruhengeri, and Cyangugu began almost simultaneously with the killings in Kigali. Soon after, Kibuye began the massacres. Kibungo and Gikongoro were the scenes of some of the most horrific killings during the genocide. The Bugesera region in Kigali *prefecture* also had major massacres. Butare and Gitarama were effectively left alone between 1991 and 1993 and resisted the call for the genocide the longest. If we consider the social, historical, and political context of this crisis region by region we can see that ethnic hatred was not the major factor in the pattern of complicity and resistence.

The North: Fictions of Tradition

By the 1980s the main positions in Habyarimana's regime, as well as access to resources such as scholarships, common property, and development aid, were concentrated in the hands of elites from the *prefectures* of Ruhengeri and Gisenyi. By April 1994 power was concentrated even further into the hands of certain members of First Lady Mme Agathe Habyarimana's family and certain members of the northern elite, the infamous *akazu* (little house). At the same time, this area had one of the highest population densities in Rwanda, the greatest disparity in landholdings, and a growing landless group. The land clientage at the root of this disparity was justified as a "Hutu institution" predating Tutsi and colonial rule. This area also had the lowest proportion of Tutsi in the country, because it had been incorporated into the precolonial state only during the last years of the nineteenth century. The problem of landlessness and the growing gap between rich and poor made this area potentially the most explosive for the Habyarimana regime. The core of the extremists came from this area and this extremism favored the interests of the political elite. . . . There was a pattern of "ethnic" massacres through this area during the 1990s. In April 1994, this area helped provide manpower to help hunt down and kill Tutsi in other regions of the country.

The East: The Contested Frontier

The regions of Kibungo and the Bugesera in Kigali *prefecture* also saw some of the worst killing before and during the early part of the genocide. These areas were not as populated as either the northern *prefectures* or the *prefectures* of Butare and Gitarama; however, they were a major area of in-migration and the site of much of the unsettled land in Rwanda before the 1990s. Many of the Tutsi who fled the persecutions and killings of 1959–62, 1963, and 1973, settled into this area. During the 1980s and 1990s, many of the landless and jobless youth from the north moved into these areas looking for land. By the 1980s most of the unsettled land was settled and this region could no longer absorb surplus population. During the 1990s the old established Tutsi and the in-migrant Hutu groups clashed for access to land and for power. . . . Given this situation, the government targeted this area for extremist propaganda and for its campaign of killings in the 1990s, and found fertile ground among the landless youth from the north for the militias.

The Southwest: Neglected Terrains

Cyangugu in the southwest of Rwanda also was the site of killings in 1991–1993. There were also attempts to incite violence in 1991–1992 in Gikongoro but these were less successful. However, after October 1993 when Melchior Ndadaye [the first ever Hutu elected president of Burundi] was killed in Burundi, this changed and there were massacres in these *prefectures.* The prefect (governor) of Cyangugu, Emmanuel Bagambiki, had been implicated in massacres of Tutsi in Bugesera in 1992 and 1993 and had been involved in the killings of both Tutsi and Hutu opposition members in Cyangugu during 1993. As soon as Habyarimana's airplane was shot down, the killings began in both *prefectures* The west of Cyangugu, near the Zaïrian border, was the worst area for killing outside of Kigali in the first days. As in the rest of the country, the witnesses interviewed in both *prefectures* dwelt on the role of extremist politicians, government functionaries, militias, soldiers, and police in leading the killings. The "ancient hatreds" argument holds little water in this region; as [Catherine] Newbury documents, it was an area where the old Tutsi state had not consolidated power. [Scholar] Johan Pottier has suggested that the government fostered extremist politics and appointed an extremist *préfet* [prefect] because of the strategic location of Cyangugu. It sits on a major route out of the country.

Gikongoro was a site of the "earliest as well as some of the worst massacres in the genocide" [according to Human Rights Watch]. The Human Rights Watch authors emphasize that the *prefecture* was created after independence by linking Tutsi-dominated areas with an area of highlands populated by Hutu that had had Tutsi-dominated political rule imposed during the European colonial period, making this region both volatile and lacking in history and cohesiveness. It was an area neglected by both of the republics; few of the resources of the state and the development apparatus were available to the inhabitants. It was also an area of poor soils and extreme poverty, even in a country marked by pervasive poverty. It was also an area that saw a huge influx of Burundian refugees after the assassination of the Burundian president, Ndadaye, which further radicalized the local population.

The political record during the genocide was very mixed. Although the MRND, Habyarimana's party, was very unpopular in this area, nevertheless there were two powerful men able to force a quick response to the call for the extermination of the Tutsi. The MRND prefects and a number of majors, who held power under the genocidal regime, however, tried to mitigate these policies ineffectually. This area was ripe for violence and easily found recruits for the militias and killing parties among the poor and the refugees. These groups were used to "export" violence into the regions of Gitarama and Butare, which were resisting the order to kill. Political neglect and poverty played a powerful part in ensuring complicity with the genocide in Gikongoro. The anti-Tutsi rhetoric and policies of the interim government found fertile ground in this *prefecture*.

The Center and South:
The Core of the Kingdom

If the "ethnic violence" and "ancient hatreds" arguments are to be born out, then the center of the old kingdom, the *prefectures* of Butare and Gitarama should have shown the greatest degree of violence. However, this was the area that most strongly resisted the orders to kill during the first weeks of the genocide. Nor did it have any ethnic or political clashes in the 1991–1993 period. It took until April 18, 1994 for the killings to start and, in the end, the Interahamwe [a mostly-Hutu rebel militia believed to have carried out much of the genocide killings] and presidential guards had to be brought in from Kigali and the north to force people to kill. Butare and Gitarama were the center of opposition to the northern-dominated government, and the local government was dominated by opposition members, with the notable exception of certain *communes*. There was more intermarriage between Tutsi and Hutu, and much more contact between ethnic groups. Survivors spoke of the solidarity between Hutu and Tutsi, which needed to be destroyed in order that the killings could be effected. This solidarity, coupled with opposition to the killings by the prefect, meant that even extremist politicians and Interahamwe in the *communes* were unable to act effectively on the orders to kill, although there were pockets of violence throughout the *prefecture*. It was only when the prefect was killed by the army that the broad-based killings began. Again, the political opposition, the people who refused to give the orders, or those who helped Tutsi escape, were hunted down and killed along with the Tutsi.

Violence and Political Manipulation

The orchestrated nature of the killings is shown graphically in the statements collected by African Rights and Human

Rights Watch/Africa. These statements also show how various Hutu functionaries tried to stop the killings only to be overridden and often killed. More than anything, this ethnic violence represented a struggle between elites, as Josephine Mukandori, a survivor, tells us,

> In our sector [Kareba, Butare] and . . . in Ntyazo [Butare],Tutsis and Hutus fought together. . . . The Hutus who really fought on our side were the ordinary people, not the educated ones. . . . These ones who understood the politics of the attacks explained to the ordinary Hutus what was taking place and they began to desert us.

She argues that the local population was able to hold out against the Interahamwe because the militias were armed only with machetes and clubs. The Interahamwe were able to start killing only once the soldiers arrived.

Throughout the country the so-called spontaneous violence can be shown to have been systematic and cold-blooded. It did not arise out of ancient hatreds but through overt political manipulation, ruthlessly orchestrated by a morally bankrupt elite. Factors such as the growing landlessness, disparities between rich and poor, the ambitions of an increasingly ruthless elite losing their grip on power, regional politics, and regional dynamics played a central role in the genocide and political slaughter. There is no doubt there was a difference in how Hutu and Tutsi were treated—nonpolitical Hutu were terrorized while nonpolitical Tutsi were killed—but, as [scholar] Filip Reyntjens argues, the socioeconomic aspects of the killings also should not be ignored. As the killings gained momentum, the violence became more complex and less linked to purely political ends. There was outright robbery. Personal vendettas were settled. Property under dispute could be appropriated by one claimant from another on the basis of accusations. Human Rights Watch/Africa points out repeatedly that political authorities needed to chastise the mobs for looting without killing. People who had excited the jealousy of their neighbors by being marginally more affluent were attacked. As [writer] Josephine Mukandori tells us, "in the end the population lost."

3

Tutsi Favoritism by the Catholic Church Contributed to the Genocide

Todd Salzman

The Roman Catholic Church first sent missionaries to Rwanda in 1900. These missionaries were called the White Fathers by the Rwandan people, and Tutsi chiefs required that they limit their interactions with the Hutu people. Nonetheless, many Hutu peasants became converts to Catholicism, and it was not until the 1920s that the first members of the Tutsi ruling class converted. Tutsi king Mutara Rudahigwa's conversion in 1931 led to a rush of Tutsi conversions, and the once poor Hutu-dominated Catholic Church quickly became an elite Tutsi-dominated Catholic Church. In this selection, Todd Salzman, assistant professor of theology at Creighton University in Nebraska and author of several books on the current state of Catholicism, argues that the Catholic Church's continued preference for the Tutsi elite led to increased strife between the Hutu and Tutsi people that eventually escalated into the genocide. One way the Catholic Church showed this favoritism was by giving the Tutsis access to education while depriving the Hutus of the same opportunity. The better-educated Tutsis were then able to assume more power and authority in the Rwandan government.

The division between the two ethnicities became further entrenched. Salzman closes this piece with a reference to a 1991 letter issued by the Catholic bishops of Rwanda, in which

Todd Salzman, "Catholicism and Colonialism: The Church's Failure in Rwanda," *Commonweal*, vol. 124, May 23, 1997, p. 17. Copyright © 1997 by Commonweal Publishing Co., Inc. Reproduced by permission.

they admit that the Catholic Church had perpetuated the Tutsi and Hutu divide. Unfortunately, this acknowledgement did not prevent the genocide from occurring.

O n April 6, 1994, two ground-to-air missiles struck the jet carrying Presidents Juvénal Habyarimana of Rwanda and Cyprien Ntaryamira of Burundi. All on board were killed. Within hours, a killing rampage erupted in Rwanda that, over the next three months, would leave between half a million and a million dead. It is by no means insignificant that some of the first victims were Catholic priests, lay workers, and young retreatants at the Centre Christus in Kigali, Rwanda, and that attacks on the church continued throughout the massacres. Startingly, a majority of the killings in the genocide even took place within church buildings: Hutu militia turned these traditional places of refuge into mass Tutsi graves; the buildings were also frequently desecrated. As a result, analyses initially focused on a persecuted church. But since approximately 90 percent of the Rwandan population is Christian—Tutsi and Hutu alike—the focus has turned to the question of a church of persecutors.

Clearly, many Christians participated in the massacres. There were also, however, many priests, nuns, and lay people who risked their lives or died protecting those in danger. The church, therefore, was one of both saints and sinners. But did it sin more than it was sinned against? It is my contention that, in Rwanda, ethnicity—and not Christianity—was the principal factor driving the killings. But the church was guilty of complicity whenever it sharpened ethnic division through educational bias or political preference for a clearly racist regime, or remained silent before clear discrimination and violations of social justice. Perhaps what the Rwandan genocide calls most into question concerning the role of the church is its method of evangelization and the ethnic divisions it hardened and perpetuated. This complicity made it a target for disdain and retribution.

Ethnic Distinctions
The evolution of ethnicity and the distinction between Hutu and Tutsi is a central factor of Rwandan history and

was the predominant impetus for the genocide. These divisions, however, were not entrenched in precolonial Rwandan society. The earliest observers recognized two predominant groups, the cattle-owning Tutsi and the farming Hutu. Although these two groups shared the same language and culture, the Tutsi were considered the elite in Rwandan society, as cattle were a sign of wealth. The minority Tutsi, who arrived in present-day Rwanda around the thirteenth century, gradually established monarchical control over the majority Hutu. But to preserve the peace, certain Hutu were allowed to function within the monarchy. Strict differentiation along ethnic lines developed only after the arrival of German and Belgian colonialists in the late nineteenth and early twentieth centuries.

The colonialists justified and consolidated the rule of the Tutsi elite; they did not create the distinction between Hutu and Tutsi, but aggravated it. Following the defeat of Germany in World War I, the League of Nations [an international organization set up to settle disputes between countries] gave Rwanda to Belgium as a "gift" to administer. Belgium decided upon a policy of indirect rule and favored the Tutsi—taller, thinner, and lighter in color—over the Hutu. The Belgians centralized power in a single chief and gave the Tutsi control of the judicial system. As a result, the majority Hutu were excluded from participation in Rwandan politics. The ideology supporting this ethnic differentiation was that certain races were born to rule whereas others were born to be ruled. Known as the "Hamitic theory," it was based on a tradition of Old Testament exegesis identifying the descendants of Ham—Noah's son cursed for his sinfulness—as dark-skinned Africans. The "Hamitic theory" was originally used to justify slavery and racism against all blacks, but revised to justify favoritism by the colonial powers—and the church—of the lighter-skinned Tutsi. They were cast as divinely instituted rulers.

The First Missionaries Arrive

The first [Catholic] missionaries of Africa, the White Fathers, had arrived to a lukewarm welcome in Nyanza, Rwanda, in 1900. The Tutsi chiefs and policy makers were agreed that the missionaries should be limited to interaction with the Hutu; in fact, not until the mid-1920s did a single member of the ruling Tutsi class convert, and the early converts to Christianity were predominantly Hutu peasants. But this process of evangelization went against the White Fathers' mandate to evangelize from the top down—to convert the purportedly superior Tutsi first. For the Catholic missionaries, this topdown approach was the typical method of evangelization; that it did not work in Rwanda was a frustration and a challenge.

In a short period of time the Hutu-Catholic church of the poor became the Tutsi-Catholic church of the ruling elite.

Initially, the Tutsi perceived the missionaries as a threat to their established power. In 1907, however, this perception began to shift with the arrival in Rwanda of White Father Leon Classe, a staunch advocate of the hierarchical method of evangelization. Classe believed that the success of the Rwandan mission depended upon the conversion of the Tutsi; though he did not oppose Hutu advancement per se, in his stance for a Tutsi-led church he applied the "Hamitic theory" to theology. When tensions arose within the mission itself over its responsibilities, Classe's argument was decisive: "You must choose the [Tutsi] . . . because the government will probably refuse [Hutu] teachers. . . . In the government the positions in every branch of the administration, even the unimportant ones, will be reserved henceforth for young [Tutsi]." Classe's statement foreshadows the marriage between church and state that was destined to aggravate growing ethnic divisions in Rwanda. The means of bringing about this marriage was, principally, education.

Prior to Classe's arrival, the White Fathers had resigned themselves to establishing an indigenous Hutu church—a goal which required educated clergy. But though there were Hutu ordinations, the vast majority of candidates abandoned the seminaries. With their education, however, many Hutu were able to attain positions as teachers and administrators within the colonial system, thus upsetting the social hierarchy and legitimating Tutsi suspicion of the missions. This might have been the legacy—or the end—of Christianity in Rwanda; but the conversion and enthronement of Tutsi King Mutara Rudahigwa as Mutara III in 1931 quelled social instability and set church and state on another course.

King Rudahigwa Converts

Rudahigwa's conversion sparked *la tornade*, the rush of Tutsi converts to Christianity. With his conversion, conditions turned favorable for evangelization through the chiefs to the masses. Rwanda's social structure was conducive to this method: Once the leaders converted, there was social pressure for the masses to convert as well. As the sociologist Ian Linden has noted, "[I]n a remarkable way, Catholicism became 'traditional' the moment the Tutsi were baptized in large numbers." And not only did it become traditional, but it also became the state religion. In a short period of time the Hutu-Catholic church of the poor became the Tutsi-Catholic church of the ruling elite.

As a consequence of this state of affairs, many of the converts were ill-prepared and drawn into the church for questionable motives such as social and economic benefits. The Catholic church took control of education in the 1930s and exercised a clear bias for the Tutsi, who thereby acquired a monopoly on positions of authority and control, not only in industry but in the political bureaucracy as well. The sociologist Catherine Newbury has affirmed that this educational policy resulted in "clear discrimination against Hutu in most of Rwanda's Catholic mission schools." The alliance between church and state "introduced a more marked stratification between ethnic groups than had existed in the past. And as stratification was intensified, ethnic distinctions were sharpened." The mission schools' bias in favor of the Tutsi against the Hutu—sometimes even minimal height levels were enforced—was a major factor in hardening ethnic divisions and spurring resentment.

The Hutus Begin to Gain Power

The Tutsi church-state alliance started to come apart after World War II, when colonial political and religious support for the Tutsi was gradually transferred to the Hutu. Several factors account for this shift. First, Belgium's exploitation of Rwanda during the war generated anticolonialist sentiment, and the empowered Tutsi began to rail at their colonial yoke. Because of the alliance between church and state, the church was also implicated in this discontent. Second, the champion of a Tutsi-dominated church, Father Classe, died in 1945. (According to the historian Gerard Prunier, Classe was "almost a national monument" for his influence on

Rwandan politics.) He was replaced by the White Father Laurent Deprimoz, who began to address the divisive nature of ethnicity within the Rwandan church. Perhaps inevitably, however, Deprimoz's efforts backfired and only made these divisions more strident. Third, the number of indigenous clergy, the majority of whom were Tutsi, came to equal the number of European clergy, and a struggle broke out for control of the church. The imbalance of power between the White Fathers and indigenous clergy caused no little resentment among the latter. This struggle was intensified by new Belgian missionaries who, Flemish rather than Walloon and from humbler social classes, did not sympathize with the aristocratic Tutsi but encouraged the downtrodden Hutu.

The mission schools' bias in favor of the Tutsi against the Hutu . . . was a major factor in hardening ethnic divisions and spurring resentment.

The final vestiges of colonial control over Rwanda were shattered with the death of King Rudahigwa in 1959 and the investiture of his successor, Jean-Baptiste Ndahindurwa, who took the name Kigeri V. This transition of power precipitated a civil war; Tutsi and Hutu formed factions poised against one another. Pushed by Tutsi clergy, Bishop Aloys Bigirumwami of the Nyundo vicarate became the symbolic figurehead of the Tutsi faction, the Union Nationale Rwandaise, and Bishop Andre Perraudin of Kabgayi was perceived as the champion of the oppressed Hutu for his insistence on the church's social teaching. Though they had issued a joint letter calling for peace, the bishops—and church—were swept into the emerging violence.

This powder keg exploded in November 1959, after the brutal attack of a Hutu activist. A peasant revolt (Jacquerie) broke out leaving hundreds dead and thousands displaced. Thereafter, through political guile and propaganda, the Hutu nationalist movement gained support and momentum, culminating in a call for independence and the popular election of Gregoire Kayibanda as de facto president of a new republic on January 28, 1961. Belgium formally recognized Rwanda's independence on July 1, 1962, but independence brought only deeper wounds. Following it, the Hutu took over governmental positions from the Tutsi, and the oppressed rapidly became oppressors. The Hutu turned the "Hamitic theory" against the Tutsi, who were recast as "Hamitic invaders" and colonialists. Many Tutsi fled north into Uganda from where they staged raids on the Hutu, who retaliated in turn. From December 1963 to January 1964, the new Hutu government killed between 10,000 and 12,000 Tutsi. Extended over thirty years, this fighting and repression constituted a long fuse to the 1994 explosion.

On November 21, 1991, the Catholic bishops of Rwanda issued a letter to priests and religious on the "Pastoral Role in Rebuilding Rwanda." A central theme of this letter was the need to overcome ethnic divisions. Thaddee Nsengiyumva, bishop of Kabgayi and president of the Rwandan Episcopal Conference, acknowledged the church's complicity in perpetuating these divisions by declaring, in a public letter dated December 1, 1991, that "the church is sick." Too little, too late? Certainly too little to prevent the genocide of 1994, when President Habyarimana's murder gave Hutu extremists within his regime free reign to execute their "final solution."

4

Rwanda's Lack of Resources and Extreme Poverty Provided the Breeding Grounds for Genocide

Peter Uvin

In the following article, Peter Uvin argues that a lack of natural resources and years of poverty played a large role in the Rwanda genocide. Although he believes the primary cause of the massacres was deeply engrained racism, the dire economic situation of some groups fueled the desperation and violence. He states that a sense of hopelessness among young Hutu men, who had been stripped of their rights, their possibilities for land ownership, their jobs, and their basic human needs, including food and shelter, created a current of rage that was unleashed during the hundred-day slaughter. Peter Uvin is a professor at the Fletcher School of Law and Diplomacy at Tufts University and author of many books and articles on the environmental and social crises of African nations. His works include *The International Organization of Hunger* and *Aiding Violence: The Development Enterprise in Rwanda*.

Before colonization at the beginning of [the twentieth century], most of present-day Rwanda was a monarchy

Peter Uvin, "Tragedy in Rwanda: The Political Ecology of Conflict," *Environment*, vol. 38, April 1996, p. 6. Copyright © 1996 by the Helen Dwight Reid Educational Foundation. Reproduced with permission of the Helen Dwight Reid Educational Foundation, published by Heldref Publications, 1319 18th Street NW, Washington, DC 20036-1802.

ruled by a Tutsi king. Fleeing famine and drought, the cattle-rearing Tutsi arrived in successive waves from the north during the 15th and 16th centuries. The agriculturist Hutu they met had immigrated into Rwanda from central Africa several centuries earlier. The Hutu had encountered the Twa upon their arrival, a small group currently comprising only 1 percent of the population. The Twa were primarily potters and hunters. For a long period, Rwandan society was comprised of these three groups. All three spoke the same language, believed in the same god, shared the same culture, and lived side by side throughout the country. . . .

Social relationships in Rwanda changed greatly as a consequence of Bazungu control.

Approximately 100 years ago a fourth ethnic group arrived in Rwanda from central Europe. This group is commonly referred to as the Bazungu. This is the term used for whites, but in reality it referred not to the new immigrants' skin color but to their exclusive lifestyle. The Bazungu never comprised more than 1 percent of the population (historically or recently) but they held the largest share of Rwanda's purchasing power, the most vehicles, telephones, etc. They conquered Rwanda using both force and diplomacy, creating an important, albeit sub-servient, political role for the king and the Tutsi rulers surrounding him in return for their cooperation. With Bazungu help, the central Tutsi aristocracy strengthened its control over the territory of Rwanda. Some small Hutu kingdoms in the northwest were annexed and their land tenure systems brought under the monarchy's control; other peripheral regions of the country were brought more forcefully under centralized command. . . .

The nature of the Rwandan state change dramatically as a result of these events, becoming more or less a conduit for Bazungu rule. To pay newly imposed taxes, people found themselves forced to cultivate cash crops. Onerous legislation (including an infamous forced labor law) was passed and new sources of privilege created. Those who allied themselves with the new administration, mastered the language of the Bazungu (French), adhered to their religion (Catholicism), or found a way into the money-based market discovered fresh sources of power.

Under Bazungu control, the Tutsi were given a monopoly of access to these new sources of power. During most of the colonial period, the Bazungu believed that the Tutsi were more intelligent, reliable, and hardworking—more like themselves—than the Hutu. The Bazungu instituted a system of rigid ethnic classification that employed such "modern scientific" methods as the measurement of nose and skull size and required people to carry identity papers stating their ethnicity. Access to education and jobs in the administration as well as the army was almost exclusively restricted to the Tutsi.

Social relationships in Rwanda changed greatly as a consequence of Bazungu control. They became more uniform, rigid, unequal, and exploitative than ever before. A clear hierarchy from Bazungu to Tutsi to Hutu to Twa, where each higher level lived off the lower level and disdained it, was established. The old Rwandan political structure built around the monarchy remained formally intact, but its nature was profoundly altered.

Hutus Gain Control

In the beginning of the 1960s, two crucially important events occurred. First, the Bazungu abandoned formal political power during decolonization. Second, a few Hutu educated at Catholic schools after World War II overthrew the Tutsi oligarchy in a coup referred to as the "social revolution." The latter involved the murder of thousands of Tutsi from 1959 to 1963 and led more than 100,000 others to flee from the country. The coup took place with the acquiescence if not complicity of the departing Bazungu. Indeed, in the final years before independence in 1962, Bazungu administrative and religious authorities reversed their position and, in the name of democracy, began favoring the Hutu over the Tutsi.

Independence created a profoundly new and ambiguous situation in Rwanda. The political system became inverted, with a small Hutu elite dominating the political power structure. The Bazungu and Tutsi, however, remained and maintained control of many of their previous assets. In fact, the Bazungu population actually increased during this time, and their influence on the economy and the administration, albeit less formal, remained significant. Bazungu standards of living were still by far the highest in Rwanda. This group also possessed large financial resources fed by the development aid system, which fueled a system of clientelism based on access to project resources, well-paid jobs, foreign education opportunities, cars, fuel, etc.

Many of the hundreds of thousands of Tutsi who remained were also wealthy and well educated. To deal with them, the new Hutu elite developed a policy of systematic discrimination, especially in arenas that allowed for upward mobility, namely modern education, state jobs, and politics. A quota system was installed that limited Tutsi access to higher education and state jobs to a number supposedly equal to the Tutsi proportion of the population. The post-colonial government retained the system of ethnic identity papers introduced by the Bazungu, keeping the practice intact until the 1994 genocide. The government also forbade the return of the more than 100,000 Tutsi refugees, on the pretext that there was no more room for them in Rwanda. . . .

Agricultural Regions

On the eve of independence, Rwanda could be divided into three main agricultural regions, according to topography. (More complex divisions have been constructed with the addition of soil quality, rainfall, and economic activity.) The largest region is composed of thousands of hills between 1,500 and 2,000 meters in height, cut by rivers. The average temperature in this sector is 20° Celsius [68 degrees Farenheit] and average annual rainfall is between 1,000 and 1,250 millimeters. As the country's main agricultural region, this area was, and still is, home to the largest share of Rwanda's population and has the highest population density in the country. (In 1960, for example, there were 250 people per square kilometer.) The Zaire-Nile crest, a strip of land 160 kilometers long and 20–50 kilometers wide, lies to the west. With elevations varying between 2,000 and 4,000 meters, the crest has a cold, wet climate with an average temperature of 15° Celsius and average annual rainfall of more than 1,200 millimeters. Population densities in this region are low. (In 1960, there were fewer than 150 persons per square kilometer.) A largely flat plateau takes up most of eastern Rwanda. Here, at elevations below 1,500 meters, the temperatures are tropical but rainfall is quite low: only 800 to 1,000 millimeters per year, enough to support the tree-covered savannah. Rwanda's main national parks, including

Akagera, home of the famous gorillas, are located in this territory, where the climate is well suited to animal husbandry. In 1960, population densities were below 100 persons per square kilometer and the region was mainly pastoral, with a strong Tutsi presence.

The high population densities on the hill slopes of the central plateau and the bordering regions are not accidental. The soil is extremely rich and fertile, the climate is well suited to human beings and animals (neither too warm nor too cold), and the area is largely free of malaria and tse-tse fever. The first Europeans were struck by the region's high population density. In fact, since the 1920s, the area has often been declared overpopulated. This claim was borne out by the regularity of famines: According to some estimates, Rwanda experienced 17 years of famine between 1900 and 1950. Yet the population during this time period was only between 1 and 2 million. However, by the middle of the 1980s, Rwanda had a population in excess of 8 million, most of whom were better nourished and had been free of famine for more than 30 years. How did this happen?

Rapid Population Increase

Essentially, Rwanda's population density increased rapidly over the years. The resulting land pressure led to a reduction in the size of farm holdings, which declined, on the average, from 2 hectares per family in the 1960s to 0.7 hectares in the 1990s. Farmers adopted a variety of coping strategies to deal with this decline in acreage. First, they converted pasture into crop land. In 1970, there were 487,000 hectares of pasture in Rwanda; in 1986, there were only 200,000 hectares. Over the same time period, the amount of land available for cultivation expanded correspondingly, jumping from 528,000 to 836,000 hectares. Hundreds of wetlands were also brought under cultivation during the 1970s and early 1980s; today's untouched wetlands are the remnants that proved to be simply too difficult or too costly to modify.

Internal migration, mainly from the south and central regions to the east and from all parts of the country to the capital, Kigali, accompanied these changes. The elimination, by death or flight, of more than half of Rwanda's Tutsi population, first in the early 1960s and again in 1973, facilitated this movement of people and freed up vast tracts of land in the eastern region for cultivation, land the Tutsi had used as pasture. (The newly vacated land was not actually well suited to agriculture. In fact, it has less natural productivity than the fertile hillsides of the central region. Today, however, this land is less degraded, having been used for permanent agriculture for a shorter period.) As a result of these internal migrations, population densities in Rwanda became homogenized. Migration, consequently, is no longer an option for farmers trying to cope with land pressure. It should be noted, however, that more than 20 percent of Rwanda's land mass—the highest proportion in Africa—remains part of the national parks system.

Although ethnic peace had prevailed during most of the regime, the racist nature of Rwandan society had not changed.

Given these land pressures, any increase in food and agricultural production must, and has, come from increased agricultural productivity. . . . In combination, these strategies have had an impressive effect. Most observers agree that until 1985 Rwandan agriculture was clearly in equilibrium, with relatively low erosion, more or less stable forest cover, quite high (by African standards) productivity and yields, and the potential for improved production. . . . Moreover, Rwanda's growth in overall gross domestic product (GDP) was also high according to African standards.

Decline in Food Production

After 1985, however, all the favorable factors discussed above began to deteriorate. Food production declined. Recent research reveals that "over the period 1984–1991, kilocalories produced by Rwandan farmers dropped from 2,055 per person per day to 1,509." Imports did not compensate for this decrease. Thus, starting in 1985, there has been a food shortage in Rwanda. A recent, detailed analysis of food production data concluded, however, that severe and moderate malnutrition remained stable up to 1993. . . .

Poverty in Rwanda also greatly increased in the post-1985 years. A decade-long decline in the price of coffee, the country's major export, paralleled the devaluation of the Rwandese franc by 40 percent in 1989. Coffee export receipts fell from $144 million in 1985 to $30 million in 1993. Aggregate GDP per capita decreased from $355 in 1983 to $260 in 1990. These declines substantially reduced the earnings of the state as well as the purchasing power of most rural households. In urban areas, wage stagnation and a dearth of employment opportunities accompanied a rise in food prices. . . .

The Habyarimana Regime Weakens

The so-called social revolution of 1959–61 constituted the founding myth of the political regimes of independent Rwanda. The idea that the regime represented the interests of the Hutu majority provided justification for its rule. This idea was invoked in countless declarations along with a mythical image of the Tutsi as outsiders, strangers, and oppressors, eager to reenslave the Hutu if given the chance. The institutionalized and multifaceted discrimination sanctioned by the state against the Tutsi complemented this racist image.

At the beginning of the 1990s, a combination of three factors greatly weakened the regime. First, internal discontent, emanating mainly from disgruntled Hutu elites, began to grow and spread to the countryside. This discontent often took on a regional form. Political opposition came mostly from the south and central regions because positions of power in the government were almost completely monopolized by people from the president's district in the north, which received the most public investment. Widespread corruption, geographical exclusion, and disappointment with the slow pace of development (especially after structural adjustment reduced the state machinery) fueled this discontent. An invasion in 1990 by the Rwandan Patriotic Front (RPF), a small but well-trained and experienced guerrilla army, composed largely of descendants of the 1959–63 wave of Tutsi refugees, was the second factor. Although the invasion was repelled, the RPF retained control of a portion of northeastern Rwanda and the threat it posed persisted. Lastly, after the end of the Cold War, the international community began to assert considerable pressure on the regime to democratize, pushing it to negotiate a power sharing arrangement with the RPF and the domestic opposition as a first step to free elections.

Together, these three factors threatened to oust the

regime and its clients. Under attack from all sides, a segment of the ruling clique countered with one of the oldest tactics in the book: They deliberately revived the forces of ethnic hatred. Under the banner of ethnicity, the large majority of the population would rally around the government, derailing the opposition movement and undermining the RPF. Free elections under such circumstances would be impossible. As it had been in the past, ethnicity once again became a tool for the elite. . . .

Setting the Stage for Genocide

The post-1985 economic crisis that affected most Rwandans also played a role in promoting the rapid spread of genocidal ideology. Almost all socio-professional groups were suffering ill effects, and, for many, quality of life had taken a distinct downturn. Young men without an education had no hope of securing jobs; even low-paid jobs were disappearing. Rural employment opportunities, whether on- or off-farm, also seemed to be vanishing. Hatred of "the other" provided a buttress for the low self-esteem stemming from chronic unemployment and frustrated aspirations. Such feelings create ideal recruiting conditions for urban gangs and extremist militia forces.

The most profound factor fueling the transmission of genocidal ideology from the regime to the masses, however, was the longstanding and deeply ingrained racism of Rwandan society. Racism develops when the objective differences between oneself and others are not accepted but rather morally condemned. The "other" is construed as categorically evil, dangerous, and threatening. For decades, Rwandan society had been profoundly racist. The image of the Tutsi as inherently evil and exploitative was, and still is, deeply rooted in the psyche of most Rwandans; this image was a founding pillar of the genocide to come. Although ethnic peace had prevailed during most of the regime, the racist nature of Rwandan society had not changed.

In April 1994, a plane carrying members of the regime from a negotiation session in Arusha [Tanzania] was downed. The events that followed unfolded along tragically predictable lines. The violence started in Kigali, spreading after several weeks to the rest of the country. Many provincial governors, mayors, and ordinary citizens did not initially join in the carnage. The interim government quickly replaced those civil servants with extremists and flew militia forces from Kigali into the countryside. The international community withdrew its peacekeeping forces, carefully avoided using the term "genocide," and shut its eyes to the brutal slaughter of hundreds of thousands of defenseless children, women, and men.

Resource Scarcity, Hunger, and Violence

Resource scarcity and hunger appear to have played a role in the genocide in Rwanda through three transmission belts. First, the elimination of more than half the Tutsi population in 1959–63 opened up vast tracts of land for the mainly Hutu farmers who remained. This land offered relief from prior resource constraints, and massive migration quickly occurred. The RPF invasion, however, ignited fears among Hutu peasants that the Tutsi would reclaim their lands. There is some evidence that Hutu extremists deliberately fueled such fears in an effort to discredit the Tutsi, continuing the regime's tradition of arguing that there was not enough land in Rwanda to accommodate the Tutsi refugee population. It is also possible that some participated in the genocide in the hope of appropriating other people's land. Others may have joined the militia simply for the opportunity to earn a steady wage or to plunder, attractive options in a severely contracting economy.

Second, per capita food production had fallen 25 percent since 1984. Coupled with the free fall in coffee prices and the reduction in jobs, this sharp drop spelled severe economic hardship for many families. Furthermore, the crisis had lasted for nearly a decade, long enough to convince the young that there was little hope of improving their lives. The organization African Rights has pointed to this general sense of hopelessness as the main cause of popular participation in the genocide.

Third, the civil war spawned by the RPF's 1990 invasion impacted very negatively on livelihoods. Farms in the northeast—a region that once generated a food surplus— were abandoned. The diversion of up to 40 percent of the government budget for military purposes drained social and development programs. (Increased development aid and military aid from some friendly regimes partly compensated for this, however.) The fighting displaced up to one million people, creating refugee camps around Kigali and swelling the capital's population. Hundreds of thousands of young men were reduced to begging, idly wandering the streets. History demonstrates that such situations are excellent breeding grounds for radicalism and violence against minorities, and the Rwandan experience certainly bears out the truth of that lesson.

The Rwandan Tragedy in Hindsight

Ecological, economic, and political processes do not form separate spheres in reality; similarly, they cannot be separated in the explanation of the crisis in Rwanda. Fundamentally, political conflicts rest on an environmental and economic substratum. Even though these conflicts may not be directly caused by environmental issues, resource scarcity clearly plays a role in their unfolding. As Rwanda's experience shows, resource scarcity can be used as a political tool: Deliberate strategies to impoverish certain groups, to destroy food and livelihoods, and to promote fear were all built on this base. These processes are not automatic, however: Discrimination, insecurity, and fear do exist in the absence of resource scarcity, and many situations of resource scarcity exist that are not used to promote violence. When resources are scarce, however, severe political conflicts and violence often have ecological consequences, making their solutions more complex. The tragedy of the genocide in Rwanda illustrates this perfectly.

Chapter 2

The International Community Failed to Respond

1

The United Nations Dismissed the Warning Signs and Failed to Stop the Genocide

Shaharyar M. Khan

On January 11, 1994, Rwandan-based UN general Roméo Dallaire sent a telegram to the UN headquarters in New York. In that telegram, Dallaire wrote that a trusted informant who was working among the Hutu command had notified him that the Hutus planned to massacre thousands of Tutsis and make it appear to be a civil war. They also planned to kill Belgian soldiers so that the Europeans would remove their troops from Rwanda, giving the Hutus free reign to slaughter the Tutsi people. Dallaire asked the UN to give him permission to secure the arms in Kigali, the capital city, and to protect the informant. The UN denied his request based on the grounds that the current UN forces in Rwanda did not have the mandate to take such actions. Three months later, in April 1994, all of the events predicted by the informant came to pass. In the following excerpt from his published diary *The Shallow Graves of Rwanda*, Shaharyar M. Khan, the UN secretary-general's special representative in Rwanda at the time of the genocide, considers various reasons that the UN did not take action even though it had this information well in advance. Khan argues that if the UN had given Dallaire the reinforcements that he asked for, the genocide could have been halted.

Shaharyar M. Khan, *The Shallow Graves of Rwanda*. New York: IB Tauris, 2000. Copyright © 2000 by Shaharyar M. Khan. All rights reserved. Reproduced by permission.

The crucial question in regard to Rwanda is why early warnings of impending genocide were not heeded by the international community with the result that nearly a million people were brutally slaughtered in the space of three months—a killing rate five times more intensive than in Nazi Germany. Could the genocide have been foreseen and could the worst of the massacres have been prevented? With the benefit of hindsight, blurred answers to these questions emerge from the shipwreck of international efforts at peace-keeping in Rwanda.

Civil War or Genocide

The critical issue relating to Rwanda was the international community's failure to make a distinction between a civil war and genocide. In recent years, murderous civil wars have taken place regularly across the globe. In Africa alone, civil wars have raged in Somalia, Mozambique, Liberia, Sierra Leone and Angola. Similar outbreaks have occurred in Cambodia, Afghanistan, Tajikistan, Georgia, Haiti, Sri Lanka and the former Yugoslavia. Genocide, on the other hand was scarcely part of human experience. Alain Destexhe, the distinguished author, considers that Rwanda was only the third experience of genocide in this century. Thus, after the breakdown of the Arusha Accord [a peace agreement mediated by the international community] and against the backdrop of continuous ethnic strife, frequent violence and mounting tension, it was apparent that Rwanda was heading for a civil war. What the international community failed to discern was that, in addition to a civil war, Rwanda was entering the far more abhorrent syndrome of genocide. In fact, unlike Nazi Germany, in Rwanda genocide and civil war occurred simultaneously.

The fact that genocide took place is no longer in doubt.

The international community's basic diagnosis was faulty and the prescription that the [United Nations] Security Council provided was the traditional one for civil wars, as in Somalia, Mozambique or Liberia. For instance, there was a Chapter VI mandate that called for a ceasefire, reconciliation and a return to the Arusha Accords, when in fact the imminence of genocide demanded a heavily armed, peace-enforcing Chapter VII presence to prevent civilian massacres. Eventually, July 1994, the Security Council did approve a Chapter VII presence for Operation Turquoise but, by then, nearly a million people had been massacred.

The fact that genocide took place is no longer in doubt. The International Commission of Experts, the Special Rapporteur on Human Rights, and the Secretary-General himself, have all recognized that genocide was committed in Rwanda. The Joint Evaluation of Emergency Assistance for Rwanda (JEEAR) refers to the events in the following terms:

> The planned, deliberate effort to eliminate the Tutsi population of Rwanda that culminated in the massive slaughter of April–July 1994 fully meets the definition of genocide articulated in the 'Convention on the Prevention and Punishment of the Crime of Genocide', adopted by the UN General Assembly in 1948.

Unheeded Warnings

The crucial point is whether its planning was discernible. The RPF [Rwandan Patriotic Front, the Rwandan refugee militia] has consistently maintained that, between August 1993 and April 1994, it had repeatedly informed the SRSG [Special Representative of the UN Secretary General], the Force Commander and important ambassadors in Kigali [the Rwandan capital] that genocide was being planned. The RPF leadership claimed that houses of Tutsis and Hutu moderates had been marked, personalities identified and armed militia trained to start executions at the appointed hour. They state that these warnings were not heeded.

Undoubtedly the most serious warning of impending genocide came in January 1994, from [Rwandan Government Forces'] insider information conveyed to [UN force commander in Rwanda] General [Roméo] Dallaire by a senior (RGF) informant, 'Jean Pierre'. Significantly, this indication came not from the likely victims, who were prone to exaggerate, but from within the circle of genocide planners. The implications of the telegram Dallaire then sent on 11 January are discussed later in this chapter, but, it apart, a meticulous research of all cables and reports sent from UN-AMIR [United Nations Assistance Mission in Rwanda] to UN headquarters between October 1993 and 6 April 1994 found no reference to the kind of messages that the RPA [Rwandan Patriotic Army] claimed they had conveyed to responsible officers of UNAMIR. In UNAMIR reports and assessments, there is frequent mention of re-arming, of military confrontation, of high ethnic tension, of likely assassinations and of a descent towards civil war, but no reference to a planned and systematic killing of the civilian population.

"The Rwandan genocide could definitely have been foreseen and could possibly have been prevented."

The analyst J. Walter Dorn has drawn up a strong indictment of the UN bureaucracy as well as the Security Council for not reacting effectively to the clear signals of genocide that were discernible in Rwanda—Dorn points to the insider information given to Dallaire by 'Jean Pierre', RTLM's [privately owned Radio-Television Mille Collines] broadcasts that incited Hutus to kill innocent Tutsis and to NGO [nongovernmental organizations] warnings of planned massacres that went unheeded. Dorn considers that UNAMIR's lack of ground intelligence and proper political analysis at headquarters led to the commission of monumental errors of judgement, as for instance the instructions to General Dallaire to contact Colonel Theoneste Bagasora—the high priest of the genocide group within the government—to seek stability and calm and UN headquarters' advice to convey Jean Pierre's insider information to [Rwandan] President [Juvénal] Habyarimana. In retrospect both these decisions were like asking the wolf to guard the chicken coop.

Dorn concludes his severe indictment of the UN Secretariat and the Security Council in the following words:

> The Rwandan genocide could definitely have been foreseen and could possibly have been prevented. At the very least, it could have been greatly mitigated by the UN. This conclusion takes into account the information and resources which were available to the UN, its mandate and its potential and erstwhile demonstrated ability to adapt to difficult conflict situations. The UN peace-keeping mission could undoubtedly

Following World War II, the international community vowed to eradicate the use of genocide, and the Universal Declaration of Human Rights was adopted by the UN in 1948, establishing fundamental requirements for human dignity. Despite the declaration, the UN did not take action to prevent the 1994 genocide.

have expanded its activities and efforts (diplomatic, humanitarian and military) at an early stage, given the clear warnings available to it. What was absent was the political will, in the Secretariat and in the Security Council, to make daring decisions and to develop the means to create new information and prevention measures. The lesson of Rwanda is clear: we must build the international political will, as well as an enhanced UN capability, for prevention. The UN should develop its ability for gathering and analysing information, for making early warnings and for rapid reaction through deployment of troops as well as diplomatic creative initiatives. The world community owes it to the hundreds of thousands of human beings who were slaughtered during the Rwandan genocide, to try to predict and prevent future genocides. The redemption of the UN from its failures in Rwanda can occur only when the organization and its member states strive anew to achieve the goals set out in the opening words of the Charter: 'to save succeeding generations from the scourge of war . . . to reaffirm faith in fundamental human rights . . . to ensure, by the acceptance of principles and the institution of methods, that armed force shall not be used, save in the common interest.

Why No One Helped

Why, then, were these warnings not heeded by the international community and within the UN Secretariat?

There can be several explanations for this gap. The first is that the RPA leadership did not convey, as emphatically as it subsequently claimed, the indication that there was likely to be mass killings of innocent civilians. Secondly, that UN-AMIR leadership either considered the RPA's messages to be exaggerated expressions of fear, or they deliberately played down the accusations against the government of the time, preferring to project a picture of an even-handed descent towards civil war but not of a one-sided genocide of an ethnic minority. A third explanation is that the concept of genocide is so alien to human experience and so outrageous an image to contemplate that its signs were simply not absorbed by the ambassadors, senior UN representatives and members of the Security Council who continued to prescribe antidotes for a civil war.

A fourth, more damaging explanation, is that the international community deliberately disregarded the warning signals of genocide for political considerations and preferred to treat the carnage as a civil war until the evidence became so overwhelming that genocide had, belatedly, to be recognized. The fact that it was not recognized earlier may have been a result of the fall-out from the killing of American troops in Somalia. At the time, strong opinion had built up in the USA and Europe that their soldiers were not to be risked in containing 'endless African civil wars'. Except that Rwanda was not 'just another' civil war!

With chilling accuracy, like a well-rehearsed play, the informer's scenario was gruesomely played out three months later.

Fifthly, it is possible that the coincidence of Rwanda being a member of the Security Council at the time of the crisis led to an inaccurate evaluation of the ground situation. At Security Council meetings—formal and informal—the

Rwandan Ambassador regularly injected a strongly pro-government view into the proceedings, one that conveyed a descent towards civil war, but naturally not planned extermination.

Nevertheless, apart from specific warnings by the RPA, should it not have been possible to gauge from the prevailing mood that a massacre of innocent civilians was being planned? The signs that were given were not the conspiratorial whisperings of scheming villains, but public pronouncements by government leaders, broadcasts by the official Radio Mille Collines and the open training and arming of the militia and Interahamwe [mostly-Hutu rebels who are believed to have carried out many of the killings during the genocide,] all of which were portents of an impending calamity. These clear signals were being transmitted by a number of the NGOs operating in Rwanda. The Joint Evaluation of Emergency Assistance for Rwanda (JEEAR) has sharply criticized the UN and the Security Council for not heeding the early warnings of disaster, basing its main indictment on the fact that the Dallaire telegram was ignored. The report states:

> Why were the signals that were sent ignored? Why were they not translated into effective conflict management? Failures of early warning are attributable to many factors. The UN was poorly organized to collect and flag information about human rights violations and certainly genocide. There was a failure in both the UN system and the NGO community to link human rights reports to dynamic analyses of social conflict so as to provide strategic policy choices. There existed an internal predisposition on the part of a number of the key actors to deny the possibility of genocide because facing the consequences might have required them to alter their course of action. The mesmerization with the success of Arusha and failure of Somalia together cast long shadows and distorted an objective analysis of Rwanda. The vast quantity of noise from other crises preoccupied world leaders. The confusion between genocide as a legal term, referring primarily to an intent, and popular association of genocide with massive murder in the order of hundreds of thousands, created confusion. Finally, a general desensitization developed with respect

to mass slaughters, and the possibility of a massive genocide actually occurring seemed beyond belief.

The meticulously planned genocide started on 6 April. On 11 April the Security Council, acting against the advice of the Secretary-General, decided to reduce its peace-keeping representation in Rwanda from 2548 to 250. It was not until 21 April, almost three weeks later, that the Security Council, recognizing the unmistakable spectre of genocide, revised its earlier decision and decided to build up the peace-keeping force strength to 5500, although still with a Chapter VI mandate. Already, hundreds of thousands of Rwandans had been brutally massacred. It was a classic case of shutting the gate after the horse had bolted. It took a further three months for UNAMIR troop strength to build up. By then the civil war and genocide were over.

The international community's failure to respond to the threat of planned massacres has deservedly drawn fierce criticism in the media and by inquiry commissions in Belgium, France, Canada, the US Congress and the Scandinavian countries. In my opinion, a combination of the factors outlined above led to the Security Council turning away from adopting pro-active measures. I believe that if General Dallaire had been given a fully equipped force (2548 peacekeepers) as sanctioned in his October 1993 mandate, let alone the 5500-strong force approved in May 1994 for UNAMIR II, he would have been able to contain the massacre that followed the 6 April plane crash.

The Dallaire Telegram

The telegram sent by General Dallaire on 11 January 1994 to the head of the DPKO's [Department of Peacekeeping Operations at UN Headquarters] Military Division, General [Maurice] Baril, has led to the severest indictment of UN bureaucracy, notably of the DPKO's senior personnel. The telegram needs to be placed in perspective. In it General Dallaire reported that an informant ('Jean Pierre') belonging to the inner circle of President Habyarimana's government had conveyed information of plans to massacre Tutsis on receipt of a green signal. Tutsi homes had been earmarked, killer squads trained and arms procured so that '1000 Tutsis could be killed in 20 minutes'. The informer also described that part of the plan was to give the appearance of a civil war and to kill Belgian soldiers so that foreign troops would be evacuated and the field left open for the massacre of the Tutsis. Dallaire sought permission to act in order to neutralize the arms caches and to protect the informant. UN headquarters did not give the permission on the grounds that UNAMIR's mandate did not allow the pro-active action proposed by Dallaire. Instead, UN headquarters proposed that President Habyarimana be made aware of the information without revealing the source.

With chilling accuracy, like a well-rehearsed play, the informer's scenario was gruesomely played out three months later. Even the brutal murder of ten Belgian soldiers was carried out, leading to the withdrawal of Belgian and Bangladeshi peace-keepers. For the next seven weeks, the Security Council dithered, eventually deciding, bizarrely, to withdraw from the scene, producing precisely the reaction that the genociders had sought to evoke. During this period, UNAMIR, reduced to 444 peace-keepers, played a heroic role, saving lives and protecting harassed Tutsis and moderate Hutus, but they had neither the mandate nor the personnel to control the genocide.

The JEEAR's severe criticism of the UN and specifically of the Secretary-General has been stated in the following terms:

> Those charged with leadership had a distorted view of events: both the Secretariat and the Security Council drew a picture of Rwanda as a failed state in which rogue troops and spontaneous mobs were killing Tutsi. The concept of a failed state, of course, suggested the analogy with Somalia, then uppermost in the consciousness of UN officials. Bureaucratic caution reinforced the conclusion drawn from that experience: the UN could not afford another peace-keeping failure, with failure defined as loss of UN peace-keepers in the field. Finally, the striking aspect of the first week of crisis was the physical absence from New York of Boutros-Ghali, who was travelling at a brisk pace in Europe and the former Soviet Union. During the fast-moving and critical first days of crisis, the Secretary-General was unavailable to provide leadership for action.

While I share the criticism that early warnings of genocide should have been picked up by the international community and preemptive action taken, the suggestion by some commentators of a hard-broiled, inured UN bureaucracy being insensitive to the fate of Rwanda is not justified.

First, Dallaire's telegram did evoke an immediate reaction from the DPKO in that its contents were shared with key members of the Security Council. Their response was defensive, almost like a cold shower. Secondly, Dallaire's telegram sought permission to act at a military level, namely to neutralize the arms caches and to protect the informant. The proposal was duly studied but turned down on legalistic grounds. The political content of the telegram was acknowledged, acted upon and presumably awaited confirmation from the Secretary-General's Special Representative in Rwanda, Dr. [Jacques-Roger] Booh-Booh, who was known to take a different view of the situation in Rwanda to General Dallaire. No such confirmation of impending genocide subsequently came from UN sources in Rwanda, especially from those responsible for political analysis. While there can be little doubt that a heavily understaffed, severely overburdened UN bureaucracy should have reacted with greater alacrity to the Dallaire telegram, the responsibility for consistent inaction, including with regard to the Dallaire telegram, lies squarely with the international community and with UNAMIR's political wing that did not convey in a single report after Dallaire's telegram the possibility of civilian massacres instigated by government elements.

2

The Disaster in Somalia Influenced the United Nations to Delay Intervention in Rwanda

Iqbal Riza, interviewed by *Frontline*

In the following interview with *Frontline*, a PBS news show, Iqbal Riza, chief of staff to UN secretary-general Kofi Annan, responds to charges that UN officials did not help prevent the genocide in Rwanda even though they had advance warning. Riza cites the military losses the United States had recently suffered in Somalia as one of the main reasons that the UN did not act to prevent the genocide. In the early 1990s, the United States and the UN had sent troops into Somalia, a small country in Eastern Africa, in order to ensure that food and other relief supplies donated from organizations around the world actually reached the people in need. Militias had been stealing the relief supplies by intercepting them at delivery points. In early October 1993, U.S. troops were ambushed in Mogadishu, Somalia. Eighteen soldiers were killed and eighty-four were wounded. The U.S. and UN forces quickly pulled out, having only temporarily relieved the famine situation without restoring peace to Somalia. Press reports of the Somalian disaster created an uproar among U.S. government officials and citizens. Riza argues that fear of another Somalia, which he refers to as the "Somalia syndrome," led the UN to avoid taking action in Rwanda in 1994.

Iqbal Riza and Frontline, *Frontline: The Triumph of Evil*, www.pbs.org, January 1999. Copyright © 1999 by PBS Online and WGBH/Frontline. Reproduced by permission of BBC Enterprises Limited.

*F*rontline: *At the time [1993], how did you rate the chances of success with the United Nations mission (UNAMIR) [to help implement the Arusha Peace Agreement] in Rwanda?*

Iqbal Riza: We rated the chances as fair, simply because the successes . . . really depend on the will of the parties. If one or both wish to sabotage the agreement, [which was signed in Arusha, Tanzania, on August 4, 1993, in the hopes of bringing peace to warring Rwandese factions] there's nothing we can do to stop that. . . .

The "Genocide Fax"

Can you remember the circumstances of the night in January 1994 when the coded cable [in which General Romeo Dallaire, who was stationed in Kwandan, explained that a trusted informant warned of an upcoming genocide,] from your force commander in Rwanda landed on your desk?

I was in my office . . . and I believe if I remember correctly, it was brought to us by the military advisor, the General [Maurice] Baril to whom it had been addressed by General [Romeo] Dallaire . . . and we went over it.

It alarmed us, it alarmed us. But there were certain clarifications that we felt were essential . . .

Was this a normal kind of cable from the force commander?

There are a number of cables that we get of this nature, but not of this magnitude. Not with such dire predictions. But obviously this was from one source and we had to ask the mission to find out how reliable this source was, particularly since in the cable itself, after the 11th of January, General Baril had said that he was not sure whether . . . since the informant was connected to a high political personality, whether a set-up, as he said, was being prepared for that political personality. All these contradictions were there, so we had to be sure that there was substance to it. It was alarming. Now it had predicted that these killings would start in a matter of days. As weeks pass, the killings, yes, were occurring. There was an atmosphere of widespread violence, but there was no dramatic increase. What was predicted in this cable did not happen for several weeks, and I think we were all caught unawares when the situation just exploded on the 6th of April.

What did you tell your force commander to do about the informant that night?

It's not only the force commander. The title of the mission is United Nations Assistance Mission in Rwanda [UNAMIR], to assist the parties in implementing the agreement that they had signed. So, we said, "Please go to the [Rwandan] president [Juvénal Habyarimana], because we assume he does not have this information. Go to the president, tell him what information you have, and say that we will be watching the situation very carefully and we would expect him to take steps to prevent any such actions being taken, such as the distribution of arms."

As important, if [not] more important, we asked him and the head of the mission—who is the special representative, who also went to see the president—to see the three ambassadors who were very closely associated with the agreement and its implementation. That was Belgium, France, and U.S. They were actually given copies of the cable. And so the parties directly concerned in Kigali [the Rwandan capital], which is the U.N. mission, the president, and three ambassadors, had this information and were closely monitoring events. As I told you, over the succeeding weeks, there was no dramatic change in the situation. The violence did continue, but more or less at the same level.

Avoiding Another Somalia

When the force commander wanted to go on arms raid in those circumstances, how did you react?

We said, "Not Somalia, again." We have to go by the mandate that we are given by the [U.N.] Security Council. It's not up to the secretary-general or the Secretariat to decide whether they're going to run off in other directions. . . .

And that was your worry. This could have been another Somalia?

Absolutely. Now in Somalia, those troops—U.S., Pakistani—they were acting within their mandate when they were killed. Here, Dallaire was asking to take such risks going outside his mandate. And we said no.

So you told the force commander not to go ahead with the raids on arms caches that he was planning that night. Wasn't that a mistake?

No, I don't think that was a mistake. We are given a specific mandate by the Security Council. These troops are not our troops. We have to borrow them from governments, who give them in the context of that mandate, for the tasks to be performed in that mandate.

One of the tasks was to make the capital Kigali a weapons-secure area, and that's precisely what the force commander surely wanted to do there.

Certainly. He has to assist the parties in making it a weapons-secure area, not go and recover weapons himself.

But in this case the parties may well have been, as he hinted, some of those who were hiding the weapons.

And that is why we went to the president who was one of the parties who had signed the agreement.

But wouldn't that be telling exactly the person who was in on the conspiracy that you knew about it?

We regret, in hindsight, that we did not interpret the information in that cable to be the truth.

This was a Person who was assasinated so that the genocide could begin. [On April 6, 1994, the plane carrying Rwandan president Juvénal Habyarimana and Burundian president Cyprien Ntaryamira was shot down over Kigali, the capital of Rwanda. Some critics believe that the death of President Habyarimana was planned by members of his own government with the purpose of starting the genocide, which began within hours of the crash.]

But his camp and those around him were part of the conspiracy.

Oh, his camp, yes, but we were dealing with the president. He was the authority who had signed the agreement, who was responsible for implementing the agreement. We could not have kept him in the dark.

Did you tell Mr. Kofi Annan [UN secretary general] about the cable from the force commander?

Mr. Annan was head of the department. He used to see the cables. Yes, we must have briefed him the following day or maybe a day or two later.

. . . After you had told the force commander not to do anything.

Absolutely. I was in charge of the mission and I decided on what instructions were sent.

So the decision not to act, the responsibility rests with you.

Those were the instructions that went under my signature, yes.

Do you regret what you did?

Of course we do. We regret, in hindsight, that we did not interpret the information in that cable to be the truth.

Misinterpreting the Cable

How do you think you should have interpreted it?

Now, let me say one thing. We can't pretend that this was the only source of information, this cable. As I mentioned, the cable, itself, was given to various people in Kigali, various governments. These governments and other governments had their own sources of information, of intelligence. As events unfolded, what I recall the scene to be is that everyone involved was preoccupied with a political solution. A transitional government should have been established by the 31st of December [1993]. Here we were going through January, February and March, without this government. This was the first priority, and, clearly, when I looked through the cables last night, it comes out very clearly that the conviction was that if they had a political solution, then the violence would subside. In other words, the violence was not connected to a planning of a genocide, nobody saw it like that. It was seen as a result of a political deadlock.

The cable was quite clear. The cable said that the informer had been trained to exterminate Tutsis. That wasn't political, that was a kind of genocide, truly.

Look, since the 1960s, there have been cycles of vio-

In the early 1990s troops were sent to Somalia to ensure that relief supplies actually reached the people in need. Here milk is distributed to refugee children.

lence—Tutsis against Hutus, Hutus against Tutsis. I'm sorry to put it so cynically. It was nothing new. This had continued from the '60s through the '70s into the '80s and here it was in the '90s . . .

[What] of the point, that you should have seen it coming, that it had happened before? And here was the detail that proved it was going to happen again . . . on an even greater scale.

Look, this was one of the worst instances of violence and killings that had occurred after the Second World War. All of us deeply regret it, all of us are remorseful about it, anybody who had anything to do with it, and that means the international community, not just the United Nations. The information was there. There were two stages where we failed. Yes, we failed.

We were cautious in interpreting our mandate and in giving guidance because we did not want a repetition of Somalia.

One was to correctly interpret the information, and as I say, we were not alone in that. Secondly, when the enormity became obvious on the 6th of April [1994], to have the political will to do something about it. You know very well that when the situation exploded, what was the reaction? If the political will had been there, it should have been to strengthen the mission, give it a stronger mandate and try to stop these killings. Instead, the strongest contingent was immediately withdrawn and the Security Council put the decision to reduce this mission to less than 10% of its size.

Just to be clear, you were saying that Mr. Kofi Annan, who was at that time head of peacekeeping, future U.N. Secretary-General—he did back you in your decision not to act on the force commander's cable?

Yes, he did. And I think you should ask the reason why. As I was explaining to you, the troops we get are for a certain purpose. Let me read to you the mandate we were given, "Contribute to the security of Kigali through the weapons-secure area established by the parties. By the parties. Monitor observance of the cease-fire agreement and the demarcation of the demilitarized zone. Monitor the security situation. Investigate non-compliance. Pursue with the parties. Report to the secretary-general."

Now in addition, a fact extremely important, of which you are aware, was the Somalia Syndrome. We're talking about this cable having come in January [1994]. Three months before in October, 18 U.S. soldiers had been killed in Somalia and that led to the collapse of the mission. Three months before that, 24 Pakistani soldiers had been killed. Both occasions, similar operations—one trying to occupy a radio station, the Americans trying to recover arms—precisely what we faced in Rwanda. We were cautious in interpreting our mandate and in giving guidance because we did not want a repetition of Somalia, casualties, fatalities, some on soldiers that were there for a peacekeeping, not a peace-enforcement operation.

You said to the force commander, "The overriding consideration is the need to avoid entering into a course of action that might lead to the use of force."

This mission was never designed to resort to the use of force. The missions that were designed to resort to the use of force were the missions in Somalia, which had tanks, artillery, helicopters.

What was the point of sending soldiers if . . .

And the mission Bosnia, which had the same. There was a distinction between peacekeeping operations—there has to be a peace to keep—and peace enforcement operations, under what is called Chapter Seven of the [U.N.] charter, [is] where you do give enforcement responsibilities, and therefore the equipment, the personnel required.

And in the first few days, no, we did not realize this was a genocide.

Weren't you desperate to avoid the use of force because you didn't want to irritate the Americans?

Absolutely not. That was not the reason at all. I've just given you the reason, which was Somalia. We could not risk another Somalia as it led to the collapse of the Somalian mission. We did not want this mission to collapse. And secondly, going back to your question, the simple fact that soldiers go with light arms doesn't mean that those light arms are for offensive operations. Those light arms are for authority and for self-defense. Those are the primary reasons that these lightly armed troops are sent as peacekeepers and not as peace enforcers. That's a very important distinction. . . .

On April the 8th, your man on the ground told you that a very well-planned, organized, deliberate campaign of terror was taking place. He said there was a ruthless campaign of ethnic cleansing and terror. Did you tell the Security Council that?

I saw that in one of the cables I saw last night. Now, as I told you, in the month leading up to this horrible event, everybody was concentrating on the political aspects, including the special representative. I've looked at his cables, I've looked at the records of his telephone conversations. There was no reference to an impending genocide, or that these killings—this term of ethnic killings and ethnic cleansing had been there for a long time and it was adopted, of course, from Bosnia. Ethnic cleansing does not necessarily mean genocide, it means terror to drive people away. . . .

But just to be clear, you had been warned that there were people being trained to kill Tutsis at the rate of up to 1,000 every 20 minutes. You'd been warned that there were weapons distributed throughout the capital, and now here you were getting cables talking of a ruthless campaign of ethnic cleansing and terror. I mean, surely, it wasn't very difficult to realize that this could have been the start of an unfolding genocide.

. . . It may not have been very difficult and maybe we made a second mistake, but certainly in the first few days, neither the people on the ground except for that one sentence, or we here, knew that this was a planned genocide. We knew that the plane had crashed, and we thought it was an accident. We knew that fighting had resumed and we all viewed it as a breakdown of the cease-fire.

Do you think that was a mistake that cost lives?

Obviously it did. It cost lives, but I'm not sure that it was the mistake itself. . . . With all due respect, those who were responsible for the loss of lives were those who had planned the killing. They are responsible for the loss of life. We did not anticipate that this was going to happen. Yes, we made a mistake. We deeply regret it. We failed there. And in the first few days, no, we did not realize this was a genocide. We thought it was the breakdown of a cease-fire. . . .

Downsizing the Troops

When you were told by the Security Council to downsize the United Nations troops in Rwanda, in the middle of the genocide, how did you feel?

The secretary-general presented three options . . . the fair one to strengthen the mission. More than double it. And I think that it was 5,000 or 5,500. The second was to withdrawal all together, and he clearly recommended against that. He said he preferred the first. But if the first was not to be approved by the council, he said, "Then let us," (because it was still being treated as a breakdown of the cease-fire until a week or two later) "let us leave a mission, a small contingent there, to protect out political presence which will try and reestablish the cease-fire." And the council decided precisely on that and reduced the authorized strength to 270 from 2,500.

In the Secretariat, you thought it was not the right decision.

And we come back to the point I made earlier about political will. If the political will was not there when we had this catastrophe before our eyes, I very much doubt, in the shadow of Somalia, whether the political will had been there on the basis of one cable to say, let us increase the force, let us more than double it and give it a peace enforcement mandate, which means risking lives and risking what happened in Somalia. That simply was not going to happen.

I'm sorry, but I have been in this business a bit longer and we knew what the atmosphere was. Both Somalia, with what was going on and Bosnia, and may I just come back to that and speak about preventing genocide, using weapons to prevent loss of life. What happened in Rwanda was a frenzy, a paroxysm of terror which lasted three months. In Bosnia, for 30 years we watched it on television. It is there that ethnic cleansing was born, and we knew what Serb terror was . . . do you think information was lacking those 30 years before action was taken? Do you think the capacity was lacking and NATO on the ground, NATO in the air, and NATO on the sea? No, what was lacking was the political will, which was mustered 30 years later when the situation had reached a level where public opinion would not accept it. And that political will was also lacking in Rwanda.

You sat there in the Security Council watching the leaders . . . do nothing. Why were they so hesitant to help?

What we call the Somalia Syndrome. What we call the Mogadishu Line [Mogadishu is the city in Somalia where U.S. troops were ambushed in 1993]. Casualties were not acceptable. Casualties appeared on television screens . . . you will recall when the American soldiers were killed and that was simply not acceptable, and so those risks were not to be taken again.

When the resolution was given to go ahead with what's called UNAMIR II, with a stronger mandate and more troops than UNAMIR, how easy did you find it to get to that force size . . .

Extremely difficult. I believe that was adopted in May. Authorized strength of 5,500. I believe in July we still had 500 on the ground. Certain governments did offer troops, African governments. Those troops . . . we could not get them to Rwanda which you must remember is a landlocked country, without the equipment and the equipment had to come from outside. I think it was only August or September that we actually reached near the level.

By which time the whole thing was over.

It was all over by the middle of July. It was over because the RPF [Rwandan Patriotic Front] simply got the upper hand and drove them out.

During those months of late April and May, you personally had to stand by and watch a genocide unfolding, and were told to do nothing about it. How do you feel about that personally?

We were all horrified by what was going on the ground. We felt impotent to stop it. We were deeply distressed, yes, but again I must insist that what you are saying is that we should have saved Rwanda from itself, in the words of the secretary-general—it was Rwandese who planned the genocide, it was Rwandese who carried it out. It was Rwandese who, sadly, were the victims. We happened to be there on a peacekeeping mandate. Our mandate was not to anticipate and prevent genocide. Our people on the ground, as I said, they are lightly equipped troops under a very courageous commander did what they could. They did the best they could. They saved lives. When the killing actually started, they could not save every life in Rwanda.

Could they have saved more?

Given what they had, I do not believe so. It comes back to political will. If the political will is there, yes, anything can be done. If the political will is there, troops, APCs [All Personnel Carriers] and tanks can be airlifted in a matter of two days. This is not to criticize the Security Council. It is understandable that after what had happened just a few months before in Somalia, there was no will to take on another such risk and have more casualties.

3

Bystanders to Genocide: Why the United States Let the Rwandan Tragedy Happen

Samantha Power

In the following excerpt, Samantha Power, lecturer in public policy at Harvard University and author of *"A Problem from Hell": America and the Age of Genocide*, argues that U.S. government officials were warned that a killing campaign in Rwanda might be imminent, and did not try to stop the genocide once it began. U.S. officials received daily and hourly reports on the massacres but instead of sending in troops, quibbled over the word genocide. If the massacres in Rwanda had been labeled genocide, then, according to the Genocide Convention of 1948, the United States would have been bound to take steps to suppress the killing. Instead, the violence was considered a "civil war," so that the United States would be seen to have no obligation, and maybe even no business, going into Rwanda. Power describes the obvious indifference of U.S. officials to the fate of the Rwandan people. U.S. president Bill Clinton never even assembled his cabinet to explore policy options. Reflecting on what could have and should have been done to prevent the genocide from taking place, Power ultimately asserts that the decision not to help the Tutsi people was made largely because U.S. officials did not believe U.S. interests were at stake in Rwanda and knew that while intervention would be risky, they would pay no political price for standing idly by. This piece is a heavily edited excerpt from Power's article, "Bystanders to Genocide: Why the United States Let the Rwandan Tragedy Happen," from the *Atlantic Monthly*, September 2001. Large portions of the original text have been omitted due to space considerations.

In the course of a hundred days in 1994 the Hutu government of Rwanda and its extremist allies very nearly succeeded in exterminating the country's Tutsi minority. Using firearms, machetes, and a variety of garden implements, Hutu militiamen, soldiers, and ordinary citizens murdered some 800,000 Tutsi and politically moderate Hutu. It was the fastest, most efficient killing spree of the twentieth century.

A few years later, in a series in *The New Yorker* [magazine], Philip Gourevitch recounted in horrific detail the story of the genocide and the world's failure to stop it. President Bill Clinton, a famously avid reader, expressed shock. He sent copies of Gourevitch's articles to his second-term national-security adviser, Sandy Berger. The articles bore confused, angry, searching queries in the margins. "Is what he's saying true?" Clinton wrote with a thick black felt-tip pen beside heavily underlined paragraphs. "How did this happen?" he asked, adding, "I want to get to the bottom of this." The President's urgency and outrage were oddly timed. As the terror in Rwanda had unfolded, Clinton had shown virtually no interest in stopping the genocide, and his Administration had stood by as the death toll rose into the hundreds of thousands.

Why did the United States not do more for the Rwandans at the time of the killings? Did the President really not know about the genocide, as his marginalia suggested? Who were the people in his Administration who made the life-and-death decisions that dictated U.S. policy? Why did they decide (or decide not to decide) as they did? Were any voices inside or outside the U.S. government demanding that the United States do more? If so, why weren't they heeded? And most crucial, what could the United States have done to save lives?

What the United States Knew

So far people have explained the U.S. failure to respond to the Rwandan genocide by claiming that the United States didn't know what was happening, that it knew but didn't care, or that regardless of what it knew there was nothing useful to be done. The account that follows is based on a three-year investigation involving sixty interviews with senior, mid-level, and junior State Department, Defense Department, and National Security Council officials who helped to shape or inform U.S. policy. It also reflects dozens of interviews with Rwandan, European, and United Nations officials and with peacekeepers, journalists, and nongovernmental workers in Rwanda. Thanks to the National Security Archive (www.nsarchive.org), a nonprofit organization that uses the Freedom of Information Act to secure the release of classified U.S. documents, this account also draws on hundreds of pages of newly available government records. This material provides a clearer picture than was previously possible of the interplay among people, motives, and events. It reveals that the U.S. government knew enough about the genocide early on to save lives, but passed up countless opportunities to intervene.

Indeed, staying out of Rwanda was an explicit U.S. policy objective.

In March of 1998, on a visit to Rwanda, President Clinton issued what would later be known as the "Clinton apology," which was actually a carefully hedged acknowledgment. He spoke to the crowd assembled on the tarmac at Kigali Airport: "We come here today partly in recognition of the fact that we in the United States and the world community did not do as much as we could have and should have done to try to limit what occurred" in Rwanda.

This implied that the United States had done a good deal but not quite enough. In reality the United States did much more than fail to send troops. It led a successful effort to remove most of the UN peacekeepers who were already in Rwanda. It aggressively worked to block the subsequent authorization of UN reinforcements. It refused to use its technology to jam radio broadcasts that were a crucial instrument in the coordination and perpetuation of the genocide. And even as, on average, 8,000 Rwandans were being butchered each day, U.S. officials shunned the term "genocide," for fear of being obliged to act. The United States in fact did virtually nothing "to try to limit what occurred." Indeed, staying out of Rwanda was an explicit U.S. policy objective.

With the grace of one grown practiced at public remorse, the President gripped the lectern with both hands and looked across the dais at the Rwandan officials and survivors who surrounded him. Making eye contact and shaking his head, he explained, "It may seem strange to you here, especially the many of you who lost members of your family, but all over the world there were people like me sitting in offices, day after day after day, who *did not fully appreciate* [pause] the depth [pause] and the speed [pause] with which you were being engulfed by this *unimaginable* terror."

The Question of Genocide

Clinton chose his words with characteristic care. It was true that although top U.S. officials could not help knowing the basic facts—thousands of Rwandans were dying every day—that were being reported in the morning papers, many did not "fully appreciate" the meaning. In the first three weeks of the genocide the most influential American policymakers portrayed (and, they insist, perceived) the deaths not as atrocities or the components and symptoms of genocide but as wartime "casualties"—the deaths of combatants or those caught between them in a civil war.

During the entire three months of the genocide Clinton never assembled his top policy advisers to discuss the killings.

Yet this formulation avoids the critical issue of whether Clinton and his close advisers might reasonably have been expected to "fully appreciate" the true dimensions and nature of the massacres. During the first three days of the killings U.S. diplomats in Rwanda reported back to Washington that well-armed extremists were intent on eliminating the Tutsi. And the American press spoke of the door-to-door hunting of unarmed civilians. By the end of the second week informed nongovernmental groups had already begun to call on the Administration to use the term "genocide," causing diplomats and lawyers at the State Department to begin debating the word's applicability soon thereafter. In order not to appreciate that genocide or something close to it was under way, U.S. officials had to ignore public reports and internal intelligence and debate.

The story of U.S. policy during the genocide in Rwanda is not a story of willful complicity with evil. U.S. officials did not sit around and conspire to allow genocide to happen. But whatever their convictions about "never again," many of them did sit around, and they most certainly did allow genocide to happen. In examining how and why the United States failed Rwanda, we see that without strong leadership the system will incline toward risk-averse policy choices. We also see that with the possibility of deploying U.S. troops to Rwanda taken off the table early on—and with crises elsewhere in the world unfolding—the slaughter never received the top-level attention it deserved. Domestic political forces that might have pressed for action were absent. And most U.S. officials opposed to American involvement in Rwanda were firmly convinced that they were doing all they could— and, most important, all they *should*—in light of competing American interests and a highly circumscribed understanding of what was "possible" for the United States to do. . . .

No National Interest

The Americans who wanted the United States to do the most were those who knew Rwanda best. Joyce Leader, [U.S. ambassador in Kigali, Rwanda, David] Rawson's deputy in Rwanda, had been the one to close and lock the doors to the U.S. embassy [during the early days of the genocide]. When she returned to Washington, she was given a small room in a back office and told to prepare the State Department's daily Rwanda summaries, drawing on press and U.S. intelligence reports. Incredibly, despite her expertise and her contacts in Rwanda, she was rarely consulted and was instructed not to deal directly with her sources in Kigali. Once, an NSC [National Security Council] staffer did call to ask, "Short of sending in the troops, what is to be done?" Leader's response, unwelcome, was "Send in the troops." Throughout the U.S. government Africa specialists had the least clout of all regional specialists and the smallest chance of effecting policy outcomes. In contrast, those with the most pull in the bureaucracy had never visited Rwanda or met any Rwandans. They spoke analytically of "national interests" or even "humanitarian consequences" without appearing gripped by the unfolding human tragedy. The dearth of country or regional expertise in the senior circles of government not only reduces the capacity of officers to assess the "news." It also increases the likelihood a dynamic identified by Lake in his 1971 *Foreign Policy* article that killings will become abstractions. "Ethnic bloodshed" in Africa was thought to be regrettable but not particularly unusual. . . .

During the entire three months of the genocide Clinton never assembled his top policy advisers to discuss the killings. Anthony Lake [national security adviser to President Clinton from 1993 to 1996] likewise never gathered the "principals"—the Cabinet-level members of the foreign-policy team. Rwanda was never thought to warrant its own top-level meeting. When the subject came up, it did so along with, and subordinate to, discussions of Somalia, Haiti, and Bosnia. Whereas these crises involved U.S. personnel and stirred some public interest, Rwanda generated no sense of urgency and could safely be avoided by Clinton at no political cost. The editorial boards of the major American newspapers discouraged U.S. intervention during the genocide. They, like the Administration, lamented the killings but believed, in the words of an April 17 [1994] *Washington Post* editorial, "The United States has no recognizable national interest in taking a role, certainly not a leading role." Capitol Hill was quiet. Some in Congress were glad to be free of the expense of another flawed UN mission. Others, including a few members of the Africa subcommittees and the Congressional Black Caucus, eventually appealed tamely for the United States to play a role in ending the violence—but again, they did not dare urge U.S. involvement on the ground, and they did not kick up a public fuss. Members of Congress weren't hearing from their constituents. Pat Schroeder, of Colorado, said on April 30, "There are some groups terribly concerned about the gorillas . . . But—it sounds terrible—people just don't know what can be done about the people." . . .

It is not hard to conceive of how the United States might have done things differently.

The deck was stacked against Rwandans who were hiding wherever they could and praying for rescue. The American public expressed no interest in Rwanda, and the crisis was treated as a civil war requiring a cease-fire or as a "peace-keeping problem" requiring a UN withdrawal. It was not treated as a genocide demanding instant action. The top policymakers trusted that their subordinates were doing all they could do, while the subordinates worked with an extremely narrow understanding of what the United States *would* do. . . .

In Hindsight

It is not hard to conceive of how the United States might have done things differently. Ahead of the [April 6, 1994] plane crash, [which killed Rwandan president Juvénal Habayariman] as violence escalated, it could have agreed to Belgian pleas for UN reinforcements. Once the killing of thousands of Rwandans a day had begun, the President could have deployed U.S. troops to Rwanda. The United States could have joined [General Romeo] Dallaire's beleaguered UNAMIR [United Nations Assistant Member in Rwanda] forces or, if it feared associating with shoddy UN peacekeeping, it could have intervened unilaterally with the Security Council's backing, as France eventually did in late June. The United States could also have acted without the UN's blessing, as it did five years later in Kosovo. Securing congressional support for U.S. intervention would have been extremely difficult, but by the second week of the killing Clinton could have made the case that something approximating genocide was under way, that a supreme American value was imperiled by its occurrence, and that U.S. contingents at relatively low risk could stop the extermination of a people.

Alan Kuperman wrote in *Foreign Affairs* [journal] that President Clinton was in the dark for two weeks; by the time a large U.S. force could deploy, it would not have saved "even half of the ultimate victims." The evidence indicates that the killers' intentions were known by mid-level officials and knowable by their bosses within a week of the plane crash. Any failure to fully appreciate the genocide stemmed from political, moral, and imaginative weaknesses, not informational ones. As for what force could have accomplished, Kuperman's claims are purely speculative. We cannot know how the announcement of a robust or even a limited U.S. deployment would have affected the perpetrators' behavior. It is worth noting that even Kuperman concedes that belated intervention would have saved 75,000 to 125,000—no small achievement. A more serious challenge comes from the U.S. officials who argue that no amount of leadership from the White House would have overcome congressional opposition to sending U.S. troops to Africa. But even if that highly debatable point was true, the United States still had a variety of options. Instead of leaving it to mid-level officials to communicate with the Rwandan leadership behind the scenes, senior officials in the Administration could have taken control of the process. They could have publicly and frequently denounced the slaughter. They could have branded the crimes "genocide" at a far earlier stage. They could have called for the expulsion of the Rwandan delegation from the Security Council. On the telephone, at the UN, and on the Voice of America they could have threatened to prosecute those complicit in the genocide, naming names when possible. They could have deployed Pentagon assets to jam—even temporarily—the crucial, deadly [Rwandan] radio broadcasts.

Instead of demanding a UN withdrawal, quibbling over costs, and coming forward (belatedly) with a plan better suited to caring for refugees than to stopping massacres, U.S. officials could have worked to make UNAMIR a force to contend with. They could have urged their Belgian allies to stay and protect Rwandan civilians. If the Belgians insisted on withdrawing, the White House could have done everything within its power to make sure that Dallaire was immediately reinforced. Senior officials could have spent U.S. political capital rallying troops from other nations and could have supplied strategic airlift and logistic support to a coalition that it had helped to create. In short, the United States could have led the world.

The Spin

Why did none of these things happen? One reason is that all possible sources of pressure—U.S. allies, Congress, editorial boards, and the American people—were mute when it mattered for Rwanda. American leaders have a circular and deliberate relationship to public opinion. It is circular because public opinion is rarely if ever aroused by foreign crises, even genocidal ones, in the absence of political leadership, and yet at the same time, American leaders continually cite the absence of public support as grounds for inaction. The relationship is deliberate because American leadership is not absent in such circumstances: it was present regarding Rwanda, but devoted mainly to suppressing public outrage and thwarting UN initiatives so as to avoid acting.

Strikingly, most officials involved in shaping U.S. policy were able to define the decision not to stop genocide as ethical and moral. The Administration employed several devices to keep down enthusiasm for action and to preserve the public's sense—and, more important, its own—that U.S. policy choices were not merely politically astute but also morally acceptable. First, Administration officials exaggerated the extremity of the possible responses. Time and again U.S. leaders posed the choice as between staying out of Rwanda and "getting involved everywhere." In addition, they often presented the choice as one between doing nothing and sending in the Marines. On May 25, at the Naval Academy graduation ceremony, Clinton described America's relationship to ethnic trouble spots: "We cannot turn away from them, but our interests are not sufficiently at stake in so many of them to justify a commitment of our folks."

They believed that the UN and humanitarianism could not afford another Somalia.

Second, Administration policymakers appealed to notions of the greater good. They did not simply frame U.S. policy as one contrived in order to advance the national interest or avoid U.S. casualties. Rather, they often argued against intervention from the standpoint of people committed to protecting human life. Owing to recent failures in UN peacekeeping, many humanitarian interventionists in the U.S. government were concerned about the future of America's relationship with the United Nations generally and peacekeeping specifically. They believed that the UN and humanitarianism could not afford another Somalia. Many internalized the belief that the UN had more to lose by sending reinforcements and failing than by allowing the killings to proceed. Their chief priority, after the evacuation of the Americans, was looking after UN peacekeepers, and they justified the withdrawal of the peacekeepers on the grounds that it would ensure a future for humanitarian intervention. In other words, Dallaire's peacekeeping mission in Rwanda had to be destroyed so that peacekeeping might be saved for use elsewhere.

A third feature of the response that helped to console U.S. officials at the time was the sheer flurry of Rwanda-related activity. U.S. officials with a special concern for Rwanda took their solace from mini-victories—working on behalf of specific individuals or groups. . . . Government officials involved in policy met constantly and remained "seized of the matter"; they neither appeared nor felt indifferent. Although little in the way of effective intervention emerged from mid-level meetings in Washington or New York, an abundance of memoranda and other documents did.

Finally, the almost willful delusion that what was happening in Rwanda did not amount to genocide created a nurturing ethical framework for inaction. "War" was "tragic" but created no moral imperative.

What is most frightening about this story is that it testifies to a system that in effect worked. President Clinton and his advisers had several aims. First, they wanted to avoid engagement in a conflict that posed little threat to American interests, narrowly defined. Second, they sought to appease a restless Congress by showing that they were cautious in their approach to peacekeeping. And third, they hoped to contain the political costs and avoid the moral stigma associated with allowing genocide. By and large, they achieved all three objectives. The normal operations of the foreign-policy bureaucracy and the international community permitted an illusion of continual deliberation, complex activity, and intense concern, even as Rwandans were left to die.

Chapter 3

Rebuilding Rwanda

1

The International Community Must Work Together to Rebuild Rwanda

Bill Clinton

On March 25, 1998, four years after the Rwanda genocide, U.S. president Bill Clinton addressed the genocide survivors in a speech at the airport in the Rwanda capital, Kigali. In the text of the speech, excerpted here, he apologizes for the lack of response by the United States and the United Nations during the genocide. He discusses the steps that the world must take to prevent future genocide, stating that the international community must have the authority to act when there is strong evidence genocide is taking place. He also outlines the ways in which the United States will contribute to efforts to rebuild Rwanda.

I have come today to pay the respects of my nation to all who suffered and all who perished in the Rwandan genocide. It is my hope that through this trip, in every corner of the world today and tomorrow, their story will be told; that four years ago in this beautiful, green, lovely land, a clear and conscious decision was made by those then in power that the peoples of this country would not live side by side in peace.

Bill Clinton, speech, Kigali, Rwanda, March 25, 1998.

The Genocide Was Planned

During the 90 days that began on April 6 in 1994, Rwanda experienced the most intensive slaughter in this blood-filled century we are about to leave. Families murdered in their home, people hunted down as they fled by soldiers and militia, through farmland and woods as if they were animals.

From Kibuye in the west to Kibungo in the east, people gathered seeking refuge in churches by the thousands, in hospitals, in schools. And when they were found, the old and the sick, women and children alike, they were killed— killed because their identity card said they were Tutsi or because they had a Tutsi parent, or because someone thought they looked like a Tutsi, or slain like thousands of Hutus because they protected Tutsis or would not countenance a policy that sought to wipe out people who just the day before, and for years before, had been their friends and neighbors.

It is important that the world know that these killings were not spontaneous or accidental.

The government-led effort to exterminate Rwanda's Tutsi and moderate Hutus, as you know better than me, took at least a million lives. Scholars of these sorts of events say that the killers, armed mostly with machetes and clubs, nonetheless did their work five times as fast as the mechanized gas chambers used by the Nazis.

It is important that the world know that these killings were not spontaneous or accidental. It is important that the world hear what your president [Pasteur Bizimungu] just said—they were most certainly not the result of ancient tribal struggles. Indeed, these people had lived together for centuries before the events the president described began to unfold.

These events grew from a policy aimed at the systematic destruction of a people. The ground for violence was carefully prepared, the airwaves poisoned with hate, casting the Tutsis as scapegoats for the problems of Rwanda, denying their humanity. All of this was done, clearly, to make it easy for otherwise reluctant people to participate in wholesale slaughter.

Lists of victims, name by name, were actually drawn up in advance. Today the images of all that haunt us all: the dead choking the Kigara River, floating to Lake Victoria. In their fate we are reminded of the capacity in people everywhere—not just in Rwanda, and certainly not just in Africa—but the capacity for people everywhere to slip into pure evil. We cannot abolish that capacity, but we must never accept it. And we know it can be overcome.

World Responsibility

The international community, together with nations in Africa, must bear its share of responsibility for this tragedy, as well. We did not act quickly enough after the killing began. We should not have allowed the refugee camps to become safe haven for the killers. We did not immediately call these crimes by their rightful name: genocide. We cannot change the past. But we can and must do everything in our power to help you build a future without fear, and full of hope.

We owe to those who died and to those who survived who loved them, our every effort to increase our vigilance and strengthen our stand against those who would commit such atrocities in the future—here or elsewhere.

Indeed, we owe to all the peoples of the world who are at risk—because each bloodletting hastens the next as the value of human life is degraded and violence becomes tolerated, the unimaginable becomes more conceivable—we owe to all the people in the world our best efforts to organize ourselves so that we can maximize the chances of preventing these events. And where they cannot be prevented, we can move more quickly to minimize the honor.

So let us challenge ourselves to build a world in which no branch of humanity, because of national, racial, ethnic or religious origin, is again threatened with destruction because of those characteristics, of which people should rightly be proud. Let us work together as a community of civilized nations to strengthen our ability to prevent and, if necessary, to stop genocide.

Recognizing At-Risk Nations

To that end, I am directing my administration to improve, with the international community, our system for identifying and spotlighting nations in danger of genocidal violence, so that we can assure worldwide awareness of impending threats. It may seem strange to you here, especially the many of you who lost members of your family, but all over the world there were people like me sitting in offices, day after day after day, who did not fully appreciate the depth and the speed with which you were being engulfed by this unimaginable terror.

We have seen, too—and I want to say again—that genocide can occur anywhere. It is not an African phenomenon and must never be viewed as such. We have seen it in industrialized Europe; we have seen it in Asia. We must have global vigilance. And never again must we be shy in the face of the evidence.

Acting to Prevent Genocide

Secondly, we must as an international community have the ability to act when genocide threatens. We are working to create that capacity here in the Great Lakes region, where the memory is still fresh.

This afternoon in Entebbe, leaders from central and eastern Africa will meet with me to launch an effort to build a coalition to prevent genocide in this region. I thank the leaders who have stepped forward to make this commitment. We hope the effort can be a model for all the world, because our sacred task is to work to banish this greatest crime against humanity.

Events here show how urgent the work is. In the northwest part of your country, attacks by those responsible for the slaughter in 1994 continue today. We must work as partners with Rwanda to end this violence and allow your people to go on rebuilding your lives and your nation.

The Consequences of Genocide

Third, we must work now to remedy the consequences of genocide. The United States has provided assistance to Rwanda to settle the uprooted and restart its economy, but we must do more. I am pleased that America will become the first nation to contribute to the new Genocide Survivors Fund. We will contribute this year $2 million, continue our support in the years to come, and urge other nations to do the same, so that survivors and their communities can find the care they need and the help they must have.

Mr. President, to you, and to you, Mr. Vice President [Paul Kagame], you have shown great vision in your efforts to create a single nation in which all citizens can live freely and securely. As you pointed out, Rwanda was a single nation before the European powers met in Berlin [in 1885] to carve up Africa. America stands with you, and we will continue helping the people of Rwanda to rebuild their lives and society.

We have seen, too—and I want to say again— that genocide can occur anywhere.

You spoke passionately this morning in our private meeting about the need for grassroots effort in this direction. We will deepen our support for those grassroots efforts, for the development projects which are bridging divisions and clearing a path to a better future. We will join with you to strengthen democratic institutions, to broaden participation, to give all Rwandans a greater voice in their own governance. The challenges you face are great, but your commitment to lasting reconciliation and inclusion is firm.

Establishing the Rule of Law

Fouth, to help ensure that those who survived in the generations to come never again suffer genocidal violence, nothing is more vital than establishing the rule of law. There can be no peace in Rwanda that lasts without a justice system that is recognized as such.

We applaud the efforts of the Rwandan government to strengthen civilian and military justice systems.

I am pleased that our Great Lakes Justice Initiative will invest $30 million to help create throughout the region judicial systems that are impartial, credible and effective. In Rwanda these funds will help to support courts, prosecutors, and police, military justice and cooperation at the local level.

We will also continue to pursue justice through our strong backing for the International Criminal Tribunal for Rwanda. The United States is the largest contributor to this tribunal. We are frustrated, as you are, by the delays in the tribunal's work. As we know, we must do better. Now that administrative improvements have begun, however, the tribunal should expedite cases through group trials, and fulfill its historic mission.

We are prepared to help, among other things, with witness relocation, so that those who still fear can speak the truth in safety. And we will support the War Crimes Tribunal for as long as it is needed to do its work, until the truth is clear and justice is rendered.

Holding Offenders Accountable

Fifth, we must make it clear to all those who would commit such acts in the future that they too must answer for their acts, and they will. In Rwanda, we must hold accountable all those who may abuse human rights, whether insurgents or soldiers. Internationally, as we meet here, talks are underway at the United Nations to establish a permanent international criminal court. Rwanda and the difficulties we have had with this special tribunal underscores the need for such a court. And the United States will work to see that it is created.

Finding Hope

I know that in the face of all you have endured, optimism cannot come easily to any of you. Yet I have just spoken, as I said, with several Rwandans who survived the atrocities, and just listening to them gave me reason for hope. You see countless stories of courage around you every day as you go about your business here—men and women who survived and go on, children who recover the light in their eyes remind us that at the dawn of a new millennium there is only one crucial division among the peoples of the Earth. And believe me, after over five years of dealing with these problems I know it is not the division between Hutu and Tutsi, or Serb and Croatian and Muslim in Bosnia, or Arab and Jew, or Catholic and Protestant in Ireland, or black and white. It is really the line between those who embrace the common humanity we all share and those who reject it.

It is the line between those who find meaning in life through respect and cooperation and who, therefore, embrace peace, and those who can only find meaning in life if they have someone to look down on, someone to trample, someone to punish and, therefore, embrace war. It is the line between those who look to the future and those who cling to the past. It is the line between those who give up their resentment and those who believe they will absolutely die if they have to release one bit of grievance. It is the line between those who confront every day with a clenched fist and those who confront every day with an open hand. That is the only line that really counts when all is said and done.

To those who believe that God made each of us in His own image, how could we choose the darker road? When you look at those children who greeted us as we got off that plane today, how could anyone say they did not want those children to have a chance to have their own children? To experience the joy of another morning sunrise? To learn the normal lessons of life? To give something back to their people?

In Rwanda, we must hold accountable all those who may abuse human rights, whether insurgents or soldiers.

When you strip it all away, whether we're talking about Rwanda or some other distant troubled spot, the world is divided according to how people believe they draw meaning from life.

And so I say to you, though the road is hard and uncertain, and there are many difficulties ahead, and like every other person who wishes to help, I doubtless will not be able to do everything I would like to do, there are things we can do. And if we set about the business of doing them together, you can overcome the awful burden that you have endured. You can put a smile on the face of every child in this country, and you can make people once again believe that they should live as people were living who were singing to us and dancing for us today.

That's what we have to believe. That is what I came here to say. That is what I wish for you.

Thank you and God bless you.

2

Hutus Must Apologize to Surviving Tutsis Before Rebuilding Can Begin

Joseph Ndereyimana

Thousands of people fled Rwanda in fear before, during, and after the genocide in April 1994. Many of those refugees ended up in nearby Tanzania, while others retreated to camps in Zaire. The long journey out of Rwanda was not an easy one for most refugees because there were roadblocks along the major passages. In *Walk This Way: The Journey of a Rwandan Refugee*, Joseph Ndereyimana describes his dangerous and difficult flight from his homeland. He and his friends moved in and out of refugee camps throughout Africa before finally arriving in Cape Town, South Africa. In this epilogue to his short but poignant text, Ndereyimana reflects on what he has learned from his journey, including his prior misjudgment of other refugees and their commitment to return to their home country. He also argues that Hutus must apologize to Tutsis for allowing the genocide to take place so that the two groups can successfully rebuild their country together.

M y life as a [Hutu] refugee has caused me to think long and hard about Rwanda. Sometimes these thoughts

Joseph Ndereyimana, as told to Carolyn Neville, "Epilogue: A Plea to the Rwandan People, a Confession and a Way Forward," *Walk This Way: The Journey of a Rwandan Refugee*, edited by Janet Jackson. Cape Town, South Africa: Carolyn L.R. Neville, 1999. Copyright © 1999 by Carolyn L.R. Neville. All rights reserved. Reproduced by permission. You may purchase Carolyn's book by contacting her at carolyn@neville.za.net.

come in the middle of the night, at others they are in my head when I wake in the morning, while they also come at odd times during the day. I think of my homeland and why I am so far from it. I think too about how dramatically my life has changed because of what happened there.

I recall on 1st October 1990 when the Rwandan Patriotic Front (RPF) [militant Rwandan refugees] attacked towns and villages in the north and east of Rwanda, many people were amazed. This was because for the past thirty years, Rwandan Hutus had been leading peaceful lives in Rwanda, and most had forgotten about their Tutsi brothers who were refugees in neighbouring countries. Foreign countries were then considered to be exciting, and anyone travelling abroad was admired and respected. People were curious to know about life outside Rwanda and how it differed. The question in the minds of many people, especially the peasants, was why these refugees should want to reclaim their country, and why they were not content to live in neighbouring countries.

There is no place like home, no matter how beautiful or wealthy the other country.

It is important to remember that the majority of RPF supporters were Tutsi, in addition to those Hutus who opposed the former President [Juvénal] Habyarimana and who had been forced to flee from Rwanda for political reason. Local Rwandans had forgotten about those living in exile, and their desire for a peaceful return to their homeland which had been denied them by the Rwandan government. The official line seemed to be that the country was already overpopulated and that there was no more room for returning refugees.

Punishment for Refugees

Major General [Paul] Kagame, [president] of Rwanda, holds the view that for a Hutu to experience what a Tutsi refugee had endured for thirty years, he should suffer in the same way. Each year as a refugee is equivalent to two years, so that the thirty years in exile really represent sixty years of hard living. My four years in exile has taught me that these words are true. There is no place like home, no matter how beautiful or wealthy the other country. I and my fellow refugees have suffered simply because we are refugees. Our experience is that a refugee is loved by no one. People find it hard to understand the reasons why we have had to flee from our country and, because they do not understand, they treat us with suspicion. A refugee is forced to become a beggar, living off the charity of others. A refugee is alone and in despair, thousands of miles from his home, which he dreams of day and night. A refugee is regarded as a person who causes trouble and is blamed for robbery, rape, fraud, drug dealing and any kind of social evil.

I was too afraid to try and stop the madness.

Now that I myself have been in this situation, I am better able to understand what drove the RPF to resort to military force in their effort to return to power in Rwanda. They too were refugees, far from home and without any rights. I am ashamed that the government of President Habyarimana did not allow these people to return to the country of their ancestors. It was selfishness alone that made his government refuse to share the country that we had all inherited from our forebears.

If those refugees had been able to return to Rwanda peacefully, the genocide would not have happened and we would all—Hutu, Tutsi and Twa—be living together, side by side.

As a Hutu, I am deeply ashamed that I did not consider the plight of the Tutsi refugees. I also regret that as a student I did not campaign more actively for the rights of these refugees to be restored to them. I should have made a concerted effort to pressurise those in authority and those in positions of leadership. Although I did not kill anyone, I did little to prevent our leaders and politicians from encouraging the genocide. It is hard to believe that more than half a million Rwandans lost their lives, killed by their own fellow countrymen. I was too afraid to try and stop the madness.

Hutus Must Apologise

It is my belief, as a Hutu, that the time has come for us to approach all those Tutsis who survived and apologise: to say sorry for keeping quiet, and for not promoting peace. I believe that only Rwandans are able to find solutions to the problems in their country, because they alone are familiar with the roots of these issues.

I am convinced that through the love of Jesus Christ, if all Rwandans were to seek forgiveness from each other, we could then make Rwanda a paradise for us all.

Instead of continuing in hatred and fear, let us meet together in Christ and in the love that we have inherited from Him to build a better future for Rwanda. As God has forgiven our sins, let us also forgive each other. Before our country can achieve reconciliation, Rwandans need to seek forgiveness. We need to confess our failures and accept responsibility for our deeds, and in that way we will all contribute to a future in which Hutu and Tutsi can live together.

3

Women Are Playing a Central Role in the Reconstruction of Rwanda

Heather B. Hamilton

As a result of the genocide, the number of female-headed households in Rwanda has increased dramatically. The majority of these women are widows who are struggling both to provide for their families and take care of their children and household duties. Women are further challenged by discriminatory laws that constrain their participation in the economy and society. In the following essay, Heather B. Hamilton argues that despite their historically inferior position, Rwandan women are at the forefront of reconstruction efforts in Rwanda. Women have formed socio-professional associations, cooperative groups, and development associations and are actively working to reform Rwanda's legal code to end the discrimination against women. Hamilton believes that the support of international organizations for the efforts of Rwandan women is vital for the country's future. Hamilton is a scholar and coordinator for the Washington, D.C.–based International Criminal Court.

T he challenge of reconstructing the physical and social structure of Rwanda seems like an overwhelming task to most observers. The country is economically ravaged and

Heather B. Hamilton, "Rwanda's Women: The Key to Reconstruction," *The Journal of Humanitarian Assistance*, May 10, 2000. Copyright © 2000 by the Journal of Humanitarian Assistance. Reproduced by permission of the author.

socially divided after four years of civil war, followed by the 1994 genocide of nearly a million people. Huge refugee flows of millions of people and a continuing insurgency in the northwest have only increased the difficulty of the task of reconstruction. The international humanitarian community has been engaged in Rwanda, for better or for worse, from the first days after the end of the genocide. Academic and journalistic analyses of the conflict and reconstruction have been published and dissected. Yet somehow in the midst of all of the humanitarian assistance and debate, the women of Rwanda generally have been treated as just one of many demographic groups vying for attention. It is the purpose of this paper to demonstrate that women are central to Rwandan reconstruction, and should therefore be accorded more attention in the policy and programs of international non-governmental organizations, bilateral and intergovernmental aid agencies, and international financial institutions. As noted by [R. Rwabuhihi] a Rwandan woman working with the United Nations Population Fund, "You can't make peace without 54% of the population" . . .

Even women who were not raped have had to deal with the consequences of the genocide and war.

It is important to recall that Rwanda was one of the poorest countries in the world even before the genocide. Its gross domestic product fell by 50% in 1994, and it has still not attained pre-war levels of economic activity. Poverty has increased dramatically; in 1993, 53% of households were under the poverty line, but by 1997 the percentage had risen to 70%. Post-conflict reconstruction in Rwanda is not only a matter of re-building the former society and economy, but also re-launching the development project. One of the often-cited causes of the conflict is Rwanda's endemic structural poverty, and the achievement of a sustainable, long-term peace will require substantial progress toward equitable economic development. Because women constitute the vast majority of the adult working population, they are central to economic development and reconstruction. Furthermore, the important role of women in the economy and in reconstruction is augmented by their key role in agricultural production. Ninety-five percent of Rwanda is rural, agriculture is by far the largest economic sector, and women produce up to 70% of the country's total agricultural output. Consequently, women are the main agents of reconstruction in Rwanda today, and any consideration of Rwanda's future must take into account both the differential needs of women and their contributions to economic and social reconstruction.

The Impact of the War and Genocide on Women

Women in Rwanda were affected differently by the war and genocide than were men, and have different post-conflict problems and needs. As so often occurs in conflict, women were targeted because of their gender, specifically because they were women. One of the most widely distributed and immensely popular Hutu propaganda tracts circulated before the genocide was the "Hutu Ten Commandments." Tutsi women were portrayed by the extremist Hutu media as temptresses to be avoided, and the first three commandments reflect this characterization:

1. Each Hutu man must know that the Tutsi woman, no matter whom, works in solidarity with her Tutsi ethnicity. In consequence, every Hutu man is a traitor:
   • who marries a Tutsi woman
   • who makes a Tutsi woman his concubine
   • who makes a Tutsi woman his secretary or protégé.
2. Every Hutu man must know that our Hutu girls are more dignified and more conscientious in their roles as woman, wife, and mother. Aren't they pretty, good secretaries and more honest!
3. Hutu women, be vigilant and bring your husbands, brothers and sons to reason!

This document, which extremist community leaders throughout Rwanda regarded as doctrine and read aloud at public meetings, also exhorted Hutus to exclude Tutsi from all public life, including business, government, education, and the military. It instructed Hutus to "stop having pity on Tutsis" and to take up the "Hutu ideology" against their "common Tutsi enemy." . . .

Nonetheless, the Hutu commandments were translated into a program of systematic rape of Tutsi women and girls during the genocide. Many were abducted and kept as sexual slaves, raped repeatedly by their captors over a period of weeks. Others were raped and impregnated by the very men, often neighbours, who had just murdered their entire families in front of them. Certain women were raped and then macheted, thrown into massive pits full of dead relatives, presumed dead by their aggressors. Systematic rape was used as a tool of genocide against Tutsi [women], against her family, her community, and her honor. In many cases, the rape had its intended effect: women were so humiliated and degraded by the acts that they preferred to commit suicide rather than continue with life. . . .

As the large majority of the working adult population, women are shouldering most of the tasks of physical reconstruction.

Systematic rape has resulted in a number of lasting problems for the raped women and for Rwandan society. The Rwandan Population Office estimates the number of war pregnancies to be between 2,000 and 5,000, and a study by the Ministry of the Family and Women's Promotion conducted after the war in just two cities found 716 cases of rape, 472 of which resulted in pregnancies, and of these, 282 were ended in abortion. Abortion is illegal in Rwanda, but many raped women desired it nonetheless. A UNIFEM [United Nations Development Fund for Women]/African Women in Crisis (AFWIC) report states:

> By January 1995, eight months after the genocide killings started in Rwanda, at least four pregnant women were showing up daily at Kigali maternity hospital requesting abortion, which is illegal in Rwanda. These women had been raped during the war. Two had by then given birth, prematurely, and did not want to see the babies. One of these women had been raped and impregnated by the very man who had murdered her husband and four children.

Children of rape were often abandoned, and cases of infanticide and suicide were also widely reported.

Raped women also face severe psycho-social trauma and health problems. In addition to shame, ostracism, and survivor's guilt, women must contend with the fact that their rapists were often neighbours, who may still live nearby, un-denounced. A UNIFEM/AFWIC study in two health centers in Rwanda conducted in November 1994 found that women as a group—not just rape survivors—had been subjected to severe physical and psychological atrocities resulting in severe trauma. A subsequent psychological study of 100 of the women revealed that 70% of them were suffering from "severe post-traumatic stress disorders," while the rest were suffering from reactive depression, grief reaction and anxiety disorders. Women's psychological trauma is often compounded by the physical trauma of rape, including injuries to the genitals and reproductive organs resulting from brutal and frequent rape, which may have resulted in permanent disabilities or infertility. In addition, many victims of rape were infected with the AIDS virus and have passed it on to their children.

Establishing a sustainable peace in Rwanda is not simply a matter of re-building the physical infrastructure and economy.

However, sexual violence is not the only way in which women were adversely affected by the war and genocide. Even women who were not raped have had to deal with the consequences of the genocide and war. Rose Rwabuhihi, a professional Rwandan woman working with the United Nations remarked, "When you have to life with memories, it's atrocious. Most women were confronted by the genocide . . . rape, children, AIDS, loss of shelter, loss of family support networks. Life is extremely hard." She pointed out that often men can reconstruct their lives; they can re-marry, for example. Often, the women survivors cannot: if they have been raped and/or sexually mutilated, they are not desirable in marriage any more. One of Rwanda's most pressing social problems today is the increased number of women-headed households. [According to the World Bank,] thirty-four percent of households are women-headed today, an increase of 50% over 1991. Of these, the vast majority (60.8%) are widows, mostly from the genocide and war. Widows often find themselves alone, trying to provide not only for their families, but for multiple war orphans as well. Some are elderly women who have lost their whole families and are caring for the few young relatives that remain. Other women must provide for their families in the absence of their husbands who are in the army or who are in jail for crimes of genocide. Women whose husbands are in jail must also spend large amounts of time preparing food and taking it to their spouses, a time-consuming task that leaves little time for other household and agricultural duties. A 1998 World Bank study on poverty in Rwanda indicates that female-headed households are more likely to be poor than their male-headed counterparts:

> Whilst the 1993 poverty assessment noted no discern-able difference in income levels between male and female-headed households, wealth-ranking exercises undertaken by the PPA (participatory poverty assess-ment) show that after the genocide female-headed households are more likely to be poor than male. This is primarily due to labor constraints: in all areas covered by the PPA, the female-headed households in the "poor" category are those without husband, adult chil-dren, or other family labor. Children in female-headed households also have a higher probability of malnutri-tion, which is a close proxy for income poverty, than children in male-headed households.

Both widows and women with absent husbands find it difficult to find enough time simply to cultivate enough food for their families and complete their domestic and childcare tasks, thus diminishing the possibilities of the creation of surplus for sale at market for cash. Not only does this lead to household malnutrition and poverty, but also to a lower level of economic activity than would otherwise be expected.

Structural and Cultural Challenges Faced by Women

In addition to having been affected differently by the war than were men, women face numerous challenges related to their traditional position and status within Rwandan society. As in many other countries, women traditionally have re-stricted access to participation in the economy and public life of the country. A woman's value in Rwandan society is related to her status as wife and mother, or in other words, to her household and procreative functions. Women are ex-pected to adopt a reserved, submissive attitude.

Consequently, traditional education for girls did not include formal schooling, but instead preparation for her role as wife and mother. There was no incentive to educate a girl because the economic gains from her labor went to another family as soon as she married. As Sheikh Mussa Fazil Harelimana, Chief of the Juridical Affairs Division at the Rwandan Ministry of Gender and the Promotion of Women, remarked, "In Rwandan culture, a girl's school is in the kitchen." Adult women in Rwanda face difficulties finding paid employment because they have been denied the chance to pursue education. For the general population, illiteracy rates for women are higher than for men: 50.5% of women are illiterate, versus 43.6% of men. However, for the population over thirty, the difference is much larger: 67.4% of women are illiterate compared to only 43.5% of men. The women and girls under thirty have benefitted from cultural and legal changes that have enabled more girls to go to school. . . .

Women's position in Rwandan society is rapidly changing in response to the new roles they must adopt to survive.

Women also face constraints to their participation in the economy and society as a result of discriminatory customary law. Because the Rwandan civil code makes no provision for regulating property in the context of marriage, women's property and inheritance rights are governed by customary law. Women have only usufructuary rights over property, be it household goods or land, while the ownership of these remains in the hands of her husband or father. In addition, women cannot inherit property or land, which frequently leaves them unable to provide for themselves and their families after the death of a father or husband. Women's access to land and property is also particularly important in the context of Rwanda's post-conflict reconstruction. Many women are widowed or orphaned, and because of customary law barriers, are unable to claim their father's or husband's land and property. This problem is exacerbated by the huge population displacements and wholesale grabbing of land plots and houses that followed the flight of people from their homes. Women returning from a refugee camp or internally-displaced camp, often without male family-members, are left without legal channels through which to reclaim their family's property.

Women's economic activity is also circumscribed by their lack of knowledge about recent changes in the law. A royal (pre-colonial) law denying women the right to engage in any commerce without her husband's permission was repealed in 1992. However, Rwanda was in the midst of a civil war and multi-party reforms at that time, and there was no educational campaign undertaken to inform people of the change. Today, women in Kigali [the capital of Rwanda] regularly engage in commerce, but in rural areas, women often do not know that the law was modified and are therefore unwilling to do so. It is clear from this experience that changes in customary or official law must be accompanied by educational campaigns in order to be effective.

Women also face official legal discrimination in Rwanda. In the Civil Code and the Family Code, the husband is identified as the legal head of household, and in the case of disagreements over parental authority, the father's will prevails. In addition, a foreign woman married to a Rwandan man may take Rwandan nationality, but not visa-versa. The Penal Code states that a woman found guilty of adultery should be imprisoned for a year, while a man found guilty is imprisoned for one to six months and/or will be fined 1000 Rwandan francs (about three dollars at the time of writing).

Women's role in governance, particularly at the local levels, is still minimal despite constitutional protection of their right to participate. As noted by UNICEF's [United Nations International Children's Emergency Fund] 1997 report, "Female representation at a peripheral level is practically non-existent." At the national level, the Ministry charged with the promotion of women is not simply the ceremonial organ that parallel institutions are in other countries, but it still suffers from a lack of funds and skilled staff. The number of women in government is increasing, and reforms are being undertaken . . . , but there are still barriers to women's participation in national politics.

While Rwandan women face enormous challenges in recovering from the war and genocide and reconstructing their country, they also have certain advantages. Two of the Rwandan women interviewed for this paper were quick to point out that, particularly within the household sphere, women have a certain authority to control the actions of male members of the household and to determine events. In addition, women now constitute the overwhelming majority of the adult working population, and are taking on new roles and responsibilities out of sheer necessity. Most importantly, there is a concerted effort among women's groups and in the government to address the needs of Rwandan women and engage them in the reconstruction and reconciliation processes.

Women's Participation in Post-Conflict Reconstruction

As the large majority of the working adult population, women are shouldering most of the tasks of physical reconstruction. A widow's association in the commune of Save, near Butare, states that reconstruction activities in their commune are almost exclusively carried out by women. Much of this work is carried out by women's communal groups and associations.

Since independence, Rwandan women have organized themselves into socio-professional associations, cooperative groups, and development associations. However, women's associations have taken on new importance in the post-conflict society, as they attempt to address both women's specific post-conflict problems and the lack of social services normally provided by the state. . . .

The Ministry [of Gender and the Promotion of Women] has been working [since 1999] on the introduction and passage of a new law on women's inheritance rights that would enable women to inherit land and property. The Draft Law to Supplement Book 1 of the Civil Code and to Institute Part 5 Regarding Matrimonial Regimes, Liberalities and Successions is currently in committee, and could be voted on as early as June or October of this year. However, there is currently a project to revise the entire legal code concerning the land regime. This is a much broader, more sensitive and more complicated issue, one that is central to efforts to achieve long-term peace and reconciliation. There is some concern that certain members of the parliament and the government may be reluctant to work on the succession law because they want to wait until the entire issue of the land regime can be settled. In addition, even if the succession law is passed and women gain the right to inherit property, women's rights to land and property must also be assured in the land reform bill.

The Ministry of Gender and the Promotion of Women also has projects to educate people about the concept of gender and women's rights, and programs that work to defend women's and children's rights. They are preparing educational campaigns about the proposed changes in inheritance and other discriminatory laws, and are participating in efforts to educate the populace on the need to change these laws at the current time. . . .

Women, Peace-Building, and Reconciliation

Establishing a sustainable peace in Rwanda is not simply a matter of re-building the physical infrastructure and economy, but also requires the reconstruction of the social and moral tissue of the nation. Five years after the genocide, Rwanda remains a deeply divided society. Divisions exist not only between Hutu and Tutsi, but also between different groups within the society. For example, old conflicts persist between moderate Hutu and extremist Hutu who still support the genocidal ideology, and new conflicts have arisen between "old refugees" (Tutsi who returned to Rwanda in 1994 after decades of exile) and "new refugees" (Hutu who returned in 1996–97 from the camps in Tanzania and Zaire). There is even tension between some genocide survivors who feel as if they are being asked to forget and forgive too quickly, and some recent Tutsi returnees who maintain that Rwanda should focus more on the future than the past. Some divisions even transcend ethnic identity; for example, urban/rural and intellectual/grassroots divisions arise in policy formulation and implementation by the government and in NGOs [nongovernmental organizations]. It is important to recognize the multiple divisions present in Rwandan society, and not simplify the matter to one of Hutu versus Tutsi.

While most international organizations and NGOs list national reconciliation as one of their goals, and even the government has established the National Committee of Unity and Reconciliation, this terminology often falls flat with many Rwandans, particularly with genocide survivors. In Rwandan culture, reconciliation has a specific meaning that is not necessarily the meaning implied by outsiders using the term. To most Rwandans, reconciliation is something that occurs between two individuals, a process by which the wronged individual physically takes the hand of the person who committed the wrongdoing, and, as an individual, forgives her/him for her/his action. When speaking of reconciliation, international organizations and NGOs sometimes give the impression that they expect survivors of the genocide to directly forgive the individuals who murdered their families and loved ones, even if this is not their intended message. Genocide survivors speak of the need for justice before reconciliation, for prosecution of the crimes of genocide that took the lives of nearly a million people. They stress that forgiveness is only possible if the author of the crime is willing to admit that there was a crime, whereas many of the perpetrators of the genocide who are still at large deny the existence of the genocide and their participation in it. Rose Rwabuhihi, a Rwandan woman working with the UN, asked the question, "Reconcile whom? The author of the crime and the victim?" She continued, stressing that this type of reconciliation was impossible, and that the question that must instead be asked is, "Is there a way such that we can live together?" Suzanne Ruboneka of Pro-Femmes Twese Hamwe [an organization that brings together widows of the genocide to help reconstruct houses destroyed in the massacre and orphaned and abandoned children] had many of the same reservations about reconciliation as conceived by the foreign aid donors and NGOs, and proposed a different conceptualization of reconciliation for Rwandan women. She said:

> We have to ask ourselves how things arrived here. Each Rwandan must ask herself this question. Each Rwandan must ask herself, "What did I do to stop it?" Because this small group of Rwandans that killed were our brothers, our husbands, our children. And as women, what did we do, what was our role in the whole thing? Each person must take a position for the future. What must I do so that tomorrow will be better, that there will not be another genocide, that our children can inherit a country of peace? Each person holds a responsibility to be reconciled with *herself*.

Simply finding a way to live together in peace is perhaps the key to national reconciliation, and women have a special role to play in this process. As Rose Rwabuhihi pointed out, women share common problems in the realms of health, nutrition, water, caring for children, all of which are more difficult in the economic and social crises that have followed the genocide. They also share the lack of formal power within the system to influence decisions affecting their lives. Rose said, "They share these problems; they could maybe look for peace together," recognizing that, "the crisis is killing me as it is killing her". . . .

However, it is important in the author's view to avoid an essentialist view of women's roles in peacebuilding and reconstruction. That is to say, it is not the purpose of this paper to propose that women are by their nature, or essence, more peaceful than men and are therefore more natural peacemakers. Some women were victims of the genocide while others participated actively, even led in the killing. Women are not necessarily innocents or victims, and should not be identified as peacemakers simply by nature of their gender. However, in Rwanda, it is women who, often without the assistance of men, are left to rebuild the society, and they do face many similar problems regardless today, problems that transcend ethnicity and politics. By tackling these problems together, women may be able to build bridges to the future. . . .

Long Road Ahead

While the field has been plowed and the seedlings planted, Rwanda will need a great deal of care and attention to bring reconstruction and reconciliation efforts to harvest. Eighty percent of the Rwandan government's budget consists of foreign aid donations; the role that international organizations, NGOs and bilateral foreign aid play is immense. However, assistance that does not take into consideration the special needs of Rwandan women and their contributions to reconstruction runs the risk of ignoring the very people who are rebuilding Rwanda, physically and morally. International aid donors and NGOs should include a strong gender component in all of their programming, paying special attention to the new roles that women are playing in Rwandan society and designing both development projects and reconciliation programs accordingly. Likewise, the Ministry of Gender and the Promotion of Women's initiatives to reform discriminatory laws and improve the status of women should continue to be supported, even prioritized, by the government of Rwanda and the international community. Women's position in Rwandan society is rapidly changing in response to the new roles they must adopt to survive. While social change is always slow, the post-conflict crisis in Rwanda has ironically resulted in a situation not only of great challenges but also of great opportunity for Rwandan women. If national efforts for reconstruction and reconciliation are to succeed, women will need to be supported and encouraged in their new roles as heads of households, as public representatives, as agents of reconstruction, and as peacebuilders.

4

The Rwandan Government Must Deliver Justice to Its Juvenile Prisoners

Human Rights Watch

In the following article, Human Rights Watch, a nonprofit, nongovernment organization that researches and publishes information on human rights abuses around the world, investigates the plight of Rwandan prisoners accused of taking part in the genocide when they were children. Many of the accused have been held in dangerous and overcrowded prisons since the middle of 1994, when they were rounded up by Rwandan government forces. Although Rwandan president Juvénal Habyarimana has publicly promised to accelerate the trial process, the overwhelmed courts simply cannot handle the thousands of cases. Human Rights Watch argues that these prisoners, many of whom are now adults, should not be left unpunished. Rather, they should face a rapid and fair trial that takes their age during the genocide into consideration. These young adults need to be rehabilitated and reintegrated into society. Human Rights Watch hopes that by finding a fair way to deal with these prisoners now, the Rwandan government will develop a strong juvenile justice system for handling future crimes committed by children.

Human Rights Watch, *Lasting Wounds: Consequences of Genocide and War on Rwanda's Children*. New York: Human Rights Watch, 2003. Copyright © Human Rights Watch. Reproduced by permission.

R wanda is the first country to try people for acts of genocide committed while they were children. Those convicted of these crimes must be punished but at the same
time they should be seen as victims entitled to special care
aimed at their rehabilitation and reintegration into society.
Balancing the community's need for justice against the best
interests of the child is a difficult task in any circumstances,
one made particularly complex here because of the scale and
horror of the crimes committed. The Rwandan government
has the obligation to deliver justice and at the same time to
establish a strong juvenile justice system for the future.
Thus far it has largely failed to do either.

The Rwandan Penal Code defines "minors" as children
aged between fourteen and eighteen at the time of the alleged infraction, and the term minor is commonly used in
Rwandan parlance to denote people in this age group who
have been accused of genocide. This report will use the term
minor to refer to those accused of having committed genocide as children, even though they have since reached the age
of majority.

Slow Justice

Some five thousand "minors" have been arrested since the
end of the genocide, many arbitrarily, and most have been detained under inhumane conditions for years without trial. In
June 2002, UNICEF [the United Nations Children's Fund]
estimated that 4,000 such minors, all now young adults, remained in prison. Starting in 1995, the Rwandan government
repeatedly promised to bring them swiftly to justice. At various [times] it has promised to release those below the age of
criminal responsibility (fourteen at the time of the crime) and
those against whom there was no evidence, to hire and train
more investigators and prosecutors to compile their case
files, and to ensure that the system as a whole would treat
their cases as a priority. From the beginning though, progress
was slow, in part because the Rwandan government and its
international donors chose to allocate resources to other
pressing problems. In 1999, when the government officially
endorsed the creation of gacaca jurisdictions [local trials], officials further delayed action on juvenile justice.

Over the years, the government has slowly increased the
pace of genocide trials, yet has tried minors at a slower rate
than adults. The government also failed to release signifi-

cant numbers of people who had been wrongfully detained, including minors, until December 2000. By November 2001, the government claimed that it had released 1,500 detainees accused of committing genocide while they were children, by then all young adults. They were released because they were too young at the time of the alleged crimes to be held criminally responsible for their actions or because there was no significant proof against them. These prisoners, who should never have been arrested in the first place, lost their adolescence in prison.

These prisoners, who should never have been arrested in the first place, lost their adolescence in prison.

Since these releases, it has become even harder to draw attention to the plight of the thousands of young adults who are still languishing in detention for crimes they allegedly committed as children. As one report on the progress of genocide trials observed:

> After five years in detention, the delinquent will have grown up. Of course his reasoning and his behavior will have changed. Judges today have a tendency to judge him as an adult, meaning that a juvenile trial is the same as that of an adult! That interferes with the priority treatment of minors over other defendants.

Legal Responsibility of Children for Genocide

All governments including that of Rwanda bear an obligation to punish those guilty of the crime of genocide. Any prosecution of juveniles against whom there is credible evidence of the crime of genocide must be carried out in accordance with national and international law. It must be recognized that children are rarely autonomous actors in the commission of crimes bearing the gravity of genocide. It is questionable whether a child as young as fourteen has the emotional and mental maturity to hold the requisite *mens rea* (criminal intent) for genocide, [defined by the Penal Code as] "the intent to destroy, in whole or in part, a national ethnical, racial or religious group." During the genocide, the governing elite used the full authority of the state as well as several channels of propaganda to incite persons into killing Tutsi. Children were even more susceptible to such manipulation by adults in positions of authority.

Few minors are accused of being among the planners or most horrific perpetrators of genocide. Out of more than two thousand persons listed by the Rwandan government as suspected planners, instigators, and most notorious killers of the genocide, only 1 percent were under eighteen during the genocide. The International Criminal Tribunal for Rwanda has not indicted anyone for crimes committed while they were children, although its statute does not contain any limitations regarding age.

Persons convicted of a crime who were minors at the time of its commission are entitled to reduced penalties.

Yet some Rwandans in the government and on the hills believe that child perpetrators are just as guilty as adults who committed genocide. Nearly all Rwandan participants in a 1995 study by Save the Children—USA recognized that the children were susceptible to influence by authorities, politicians, and parents, but concluded that these children committed crimes of their own volition and were not forced to do what they did. In all crimes other than genocide, the respondents felt that children should be punished differently from adults, but not so for genocide. Most of those interviewed said the punishment for children guilty of genocide should be death. A group of respondents from one area greatly affected by the genocide stated, "These children, one should not compare them with other children."

Rwandan Legislation

The [Rwandan] National Assembly in August 1996 passed a law, commonly referred to as the organic law, governing genocide prosecutions, crimes against humanity, and other crimes committed in connection with them. The law divides crimes of genocide into four categories, the first being for planners and leaders of genocide, and for perpetrators of sexual torture; the second for those who committed or were accomplices in murder; the third for those who committed serious attacks without intending to cause death; and the fourth for those responsible for property damage. . . .

The organic law provides for minors (at the time of the crime) to be tried in proceedings separate from adults' trials. . . .

Persons convicted of a crime who were minors at the time of its commission are entitled to reduced penalties. They cannot be sentenced to death or life imprisonment but to a maximum term of twenty years. For any other sentence, they should receive only half of the applicable penalty. Additionally, the Penal Code allows magistrates to consider mitigating circumstances in sentencing, which could further reduce penalties to a minimum of five years (to replace the death penalty), a minimum of two years (to replace a life sentence), and a minimum of one year (to replace a sentence of five to twenty years.) The penalty for category four crimes, whether committed by adults or minors, is restitution and should not involve imprisonment at all.

Plea-Bargaining

To ease the burdens placed on the judicial system and to speed prosecution of all cases, the government has established a system of plea-bargaining which offers reduced sentences to suspects, adult and juvenile, who confess prior to trial. Confessions must include a detailed description of the offenses committed including the names of victims, witnesses, accomplices, and conspirators, and an apology and offer to plead guilty. The prosecutor has a three-month time limit to verify and accept or reject the confession. If accepted by the prosecutor, the case is forwarded to court where magistrates try the accused. The practice of plea-bargaining has resulted in many trials where a number of accused persons are prosecuted together in "group trials." If minors are involved in such cases, they are then tried together with the adults. In practice, confessions have rarely been processed within the required time limit, and at present speed many may not even be registered by the time gacaca [pre-colonial methods of bringing people arrested for the 1994 genocide to justice in large groups as opposed to individual trials that take more time and money] trials begin. In February 2002, less than half of approximately 16,000 confessions made to date had been processed. In order to ensure that prisoners who confessed in a timely fashion receive the reduced penalties to which they are entitled, prosecutors in Gitarama launched an effort to register, but not verify, 5,000 confessions made by prisoners in local *ca-chots* or lockups. . . .

The Rwandan Justice System

[More than] eight years after the end of the genocide, Rwanda's justice system is still poorly equipped to deal with the massive backlog of genocide cases, including those of minors. Any judicial system in the world would have difficulty in effectively prosecuting an excess of 120,000 accused. Even before 1994 the judicial system functioned badly and many judges, prosecutors, and attorneys were killed or fled the country during the genocide and war, or were subsequently accused of crimes. With financial and technical assistance from international donors, the government has reconstructed its justice system little by little but often has had to resort to personnel with relatively little training. For example, lay people were hired as judges in 1997, but given only six months training. In 2000, the first class of new lawyers graduated from the National University of Rwanda and assumed positions of responsibility, though few had prior legal work experience. Progress in rebuilding the justice system has been slow and inconsistent, in part due to a lack of political will.

The Ministry of Justice and UNICEF operate a joint project, housed in the ministry, to deal with juvenile justice issues. The project originally had a mandate to work on cases of those accused of genocide as minors, to which has been more recently added responsibility to address the growing problem of child rape. Its tasks include assuring that cases of minors get priority, providing legal representation at trial, maintaining a database, and drafting a law on juvenile justice. . . .

The project's biggest accomplishment has been organizing two "solidarity camps" [for ideological reeducation] and release from prison in 2000 and 2001 for those under the age of criminal responsibility, fourteen at the time of the crime, as discussed below. By the time these releases began, all of those known to have been children at the time of their alleged crimes of genocide and still in jail were over eighteen years old. . . .

The Ministry of Justice/UNICEF Project has yet to embark in earnest upon the major task of developing a juvenile justice system. The project has at times initiated efforts and suspended them shortly thereafter, citing budget shortfalls. In some cases it did lack the money but, according to some donors, the ministry had in some cases allocated the money to other projects. UNICEF has failed to require demonstrable progress in implementing the mandate of the project and, in some cases, has itself failed to provide the necessary funding. A senior UNICEF employee acknowledged in late 2001 that the juvenile justice system was still a "disaster.". . .

Arbitrary Arrests

Among the tens of thousands of persons detained since 1994 without regard for legal formalities or their rights are thousands of children. . . .

A thirteen-year-old genocide survivor from Nyamata was arrested—presumably by accident—on New Year's Day 1995. He had survived the massacres by hiding, but his parents and siblings were slaughtered. He told Human Rights Watch researchers that local authorities had summoned him to testify as to what he had seen from his hiding place. When he replied that he had not seen anything, they put him in custody. Perhaps they only meant to question him further, but somehow authorities kept him in prison and he ultimately spent six years incarcerated with adults and children accused of genocide. In late 1995, he met a group of RPA [Rwandese Patriotic Army] soldiers who he said attempted to organize his release. But authorities then transferred him to Gitagata Reeducation Center for Children, a center that housed some detainees who were below the age of fourteen at the time of the genocide. In 1998, he and several other boys were transferred again, this time to Gikondo central prison, he believes as punishment for having complained that there was not enough food at Gitagata. He was finally released only in December 2000 because of his young age. When a Human Rights Watch researcher brought the child's situation to the attention of a senior prosecutor who was unaware of the child's case, he first denied that anyone so young would have been detained at all. When reminded that the government had publicly acknowledged the detention of hundreds of children under fourteen and had recently taken steps to release some 500 of them, the prosecutor sighed and said, "There are always casualties of war.". . .

Children younger than fourteen at the time of the crime are not supposed to be detained in prisons or local jails, as they cannot be charged with any criminal offense under Rwandan law. Rather, they should go through a rehabilitation program and be reintegrated into society. Nevertheless, hundreds of such children were arbitrarily arrested between 1994 and 1998 and detained for periods of years. The youngest child accused was seven years old during the genocide. All were initially housed with other prisoners in prisons and lockups.

Among the tens of thousands of persons detained since 1994 without regard for legal formalities or their rights are thousands of children.

In June 1995, the Ministry of Justice reopened the Gitagata Reeducation Center for Children, which served as a residential center for psychiatric patients prior to the genocide, to house some of the detained children who were below the age of responsibility. Gitagata technically had a capacity limited to 200 children but, at times, has housed more. Many "under-fourteens" never made it to Gitagata at all. Some, like Jean Louis R., literally missed the bus to take them there. He told Human Rights Watch he had gone to visit his uncle in the adult wing of Kigali central prison while a truck came to take the youngest children to Gitagata came and left without him. Others in prisons were told to wait for impending transfer, but their transfers never came. . . .

Failed Rehabilitation

At first, the opening of Gitagata also symbolized the prospects for under-fourteens to be rehabilitated and returned to their families. But, in fact, that turned out to be a long way off for most. In February 1996, the director of Gitagata told Human Rights Watch researchers that some seventy children out of 163 detained there had case files. But a U.N. human rights monitor who had been making weekly visits to Gitagata in 1996 said she had yet to see a single case file with her own eyes. Although she said that compiling files for fewer than two hundred children should not be an onerous task, she saw lack of organization and accountability hamper any real progress. As the years went by, there was less and less talk about case files for the hundreds of detained children below fourteen as they could not be held criminally responsible in any case.

One hundred sixty-three children, less than one-fourth of the total under-fourteens who were detained, were released from Gitagata and reintegrated with their families in 1998. No further releases of this group were made until more than two years later.

In November 2000, authorities transferred some five hundred under-fourteens from Gitagata, prisons, and lock-ups to a "solidarity camp" in Busogo, Ruhengeri organized by the Ministry of Justice/UNICEF Project on Children in Conflict with the Law and the National Commission on Unity and Reconciliation. There the young people followed a six week long program of ideological re-education as a last step before returning home. Of those transferred to the camp, approximately fifty were boys currently younger than fourteen years old who had been arrested for allegedly raping young girls. The rest were young men who had been detained for periods of years on genocide charges. Conditions in the camp were far from ideal—two young persons died of malaria and dozens of others were seriously ill—but they had enough to eat and, on the whole, Busogo represented an improvement from where they had been before. Participants at the camp were taught about Rwandan history and human rights, and were encouraged to accuse adults in the gacaca proceedings already being discussed at that time. Many of them may be faced with the dilemma of inculpating their own family members. Like participants in other solidarity camps run by the National Unity and Reconciliation Commission, the youths were required to perform military exercises, but unlike others, they did not learn to shoot firearms. . . .

Children Released

International officials have repeatedly raised the issue of minors detained illegally with the government but rarely achieved success. In an exceptional case, Michel Moussalli, then Special Representative of the U.N. Commission on Human Rights to Rwanda, spoke to [Rwandan] President [Paul] Kagame about the problem in October 2000 and obtained from Kagame the promise that the under-fourteens would be released by the end of the year. True to the president's word, the government did release some 500 under-fourteens in December 2000. The Rwandan government and Moussalli both gained international praise and positive press for this achievement. International attention was not, however, drawn to the fact that at least 400 others who were under fourteen in 1994 had not been released and would spend another year in prison.

The extensive media coverage of the solidarity camps has given some observer's the mistaken impression that all detainees who were children at the time of the genocide had been released, including those aged over fourteen, even though thousands of such minors remain in detention. In December 2001, after the camp had concluded, another young man who had been under fourteen years old during the genocide was identified in the Gisovu central prison in Kibuye. When his existence was brought to the attention of the local prosecutor, he was reportedly released. This case highlights the possibility that others, too have been overlooked.

Justice Delayed

In order for those detainees who were fourteen to eighteen at the time of the genocide to be held criminally responsible for their actions, prosecutors must prepare case files, transfer the files to tribunals, and try them. The government has repeatedly proclaimed its intention to make these cases a priority. Yet, eight years later, many of the estimated 4,000 "minors" who remain in prison still lacked case files and had been tried at a slower rate than adults. As Bernadette M. of Kibungo said:

> The minors are the Rwandans of tomorrow but we are in prison in big numbers, and have been here for years. We need to be taught—until now we haven't been learning. There should be a way to get our dossiers done and judged. If they are guilty, find them guilty. If they are innocent, find them innocent. The problem for us is that we don't go before the court. We want to go before the judges. If we are not accused we should be released. We feel that justice has left us. . . .

Trials

Despite efforts to accelerate completion of minors' case files, as with most prosecutors, the courts have not made trials of minors a priority. In 2000, minors at the time of the crime made up only 1.2 percent of those who had been tried though they represented 3.5 percent of the prison population. In other words, minors were tried three times more slowly than adults were. As of June 2002, 7,024 persons, adults and minors, among the more than 100,000 in detention had been tried.

"The minors are the Rwandans of tomorrow but we are in prison in big numbers, and have been here for years."

The system has also failed to provide other special dispositions for minors, including due process protections guaranteed under the Convention on the Rights of the Child. Certain jurisdictions have continued to try minors together with adults rather than separately before judges designated specially to try minors. Judicial authorities also give inadequate consideration to the social background of the minor, to his or her mental state at the time of the alleged crimes, and to his or her emotional and mental immaturity and susceptibility to external influence and manipulation.

. . . Detainees, including minors, are allowed access to legal counsel only once a trial date has been set, often years after their arrest and initial interrogation. Further, not all have access to a lawyer even at trial in practice. Human Rights Watch researchers interviewed Robert U. in Gikongoro prison after his trial had already taken place.

> The court sent me a letter saying I was to appear in court. I also got another paper saying that I could get a lawyer. I signed it. I can't read very well, but I'm getting better. The chief prisoner helped me understand these letters. Then I went to court. I never met a lawyer. The magistrate did not ask me if I wanted a lawyer at trial. I went to court only that one time.

Robert U. had confessed and received a reduced sentence under the confession and guilty plea procedure.

However, the fact of confession does not diminish in any way the necessity and importance of defense counsel, particularly in the sentencing phase of those convicted as minors. For example, in the case of John S., the prosecutor recommended a sentence of twenty years (the maximum sentence permissible for minors convicted of category two crimes), yet the court ordered a sentence of five years after consideration of extenuating circumstances put forward by defense counsel.

Courts have increasingly moved to try genocide suspects in groups in order to speed up trials. However, group trials have actually led to increased violations of the rights of those charged as minors and conflicted with the supposed prioritization of their cases. Group trials can take a long time to complete, exacerbated by the difficulty of coordinating the schedules of all involved. Some groups of defendants have grown so large as to be unwieldy, such as one in Rilima in 2000–2001 that had 126 defendants including six minors. In Rwamagana, a juvenile being tried in military court implicated thirty adults in his confession. His trial was then postponed for months as prosecutors searched for those adults, completed their case files, and joined them to the trial. . . .

Penalties

The only tangible benefit that Rwandan law grants for those charged as minors is reduction in penalty if convicted. Roger M., tried after he confessed, was freed after the court sentenced him to three years imprisonment, which he had already served in pretrial detention. He had confessed and pled guilty to the crime of second-category genocide, the category of genocide under Rwandan law reserved for perpetrators, conspirators, or accomplices of intentional homicide or serious assaults resulting in death. He said he had been forced by Interahamwe [the Rwandan militia that was the main organizer of the genocide] to kill his sister's small children, in order to save his own life. Attorneys of Avocats sans Frontières [Lawyers Without Borders] and defenders of the Danish Center for Human Rights have likewise found that many minors they represented at trial have been sentenced to time they already served in pretrial detention, in some cases even less. Avocats sans Frontières represented twelve minors at trial in 2000. All twelve were convicted, but ten were sentenced to less than seven years imprisonment. . . .

Conditions of Detention

The wave of arrests following the genocide quickly filled Rwanda's prisons and lockups well beyond capacity. Conditions became life threatening as overcrowding reached monumental proportions and adequate food, clean water, and basic medicines were often unavailable. In 1995, detainees in overcrowded prisons and lockups were dying at an alarming rate. While conditions have improved since then, they remain far below minimum recognized international standards. Minors in detention are even more vulnerable than adults. The hierarchy of prisoners is well organized and, as minors inevitably fall to the bottom of it, they are relegated to the worst of bad conditions. . . .

A chief complaint among prisoners of all ages, along with the lack of justice, has consistently been lack of food. "It is up to the prisoners to make their food last through the day," said the deputy director at Butare I central prison in 1998. A typical ration was a small cupful of maize and beans per day. Adult prisoners, themselves undernourished, are concerned with their own survival, and children often eat last. Théogène N. was seventeen when he told Human Rights Watch researchers that adults would sometimes steal the children's food at Nyanza central prison.

> There is sometimes fighting for food during the food distribution, and sometimes we save our food to eat in the morning and the adults might steal it. We report it to the captain and sometimes the thief might be punished.

Visitors bring extra food, but they were allowed to come only periodically. . . .

Many minors—orphans, children who were separated or lost contact with their parents, and those whose families live too far or lack means of transportation—may not receive any visitors or extra supplies. Central prisons can be tens of miles or more each way from a family's home, and many prisoners' families cannot afford transportation. This was a problem for Butare orphan Pierre T., twelve during the genocide, from the time he was first detained at a local police station after his arrest and through his time in Nyanza central prison, tens of miles away.

> No one visits me. I don't have parents, they are both dead. My mother died in July 1994. My father died in August 1995. I was arrested a week after the death of my father. . . . The military brought us food at 6 p.m.

[in the brigade] and we also had food brought by visitors. I didn't have any visitors. No one shared with me.

At times, prisoners have gone days at a time without any food barring the assistance of family. The situation was particularly dire during a drought affecting much of Rwanda in 2000. During the drought, prison officials allowed family members to bring food every day instead of once a week, but many were unable to do so because they did not have enough to feed those at home. In cases of extreme need, religious workers, the International Committee of the Red Cross, and international NGOs [non-governmental organizations] sometimes intervened to provide food. "You hear the news on the radio," said one child. "There is famine in the country. It is worse in prison. It is common to spend three days without eating. Imagine for a child!"

5

The United Nations Is Failing to Bring Justice to Rwanda

New Republic

In 1994, shortly after the end of the Rwanda genocide, the United Nations established the International Tribunal for Rwanda in Arusha, Tanzania, with the aim of bringing to justice key participants in the genocide. According to the editors of the *New Republic* magazine, the tribunal has not only been ineffective in its mission but is also hindering the judicial process. In the next selection, the editors examine the case of Jean-Bosco Barayagwiza, the founder of the Hutu Power group, which was responsible for killing thousands of Tutsis, and Radio-Television Mille Collines, an anti-Tutsi radio station. Although his contribution to the genocide was well known, the tribunal appeals court petitioned to have Barayagwiza released because he had been in prison without being charged for three years. Following his release, the newly appointed UN chief prosecutor Carla Del Ponte requested that the appeals court reconsider its petition. It has not. Rwanda's own system of justice is also ineffective. Only a few trials have been held and the procedures used have been a mockery of the process of justice. To improve Rwanda's justice system, the United Nations and the United States must give the tribunal and Rwanda's court system more support.

Le Verdict is a Rwandan newspaper dedicated to the gruesome job of monitoring justice in the aftermath of the 1994 genocide of the country's Tutsi minority. It carefully

The New Republic, "Strange Justice," *The New Republic*, December 2, 1999. Copyright © 1999 by The New Republic, Inc. Reproduced by permission.

tracks the trials before Rwanda's overburdened courts, it runs updates on the U.N. war crimes tribunal for Rwanda, and it editorializes about points of due process. With the newspaper's earnest masthead slogan, "Justice is Dispensed in the Name of the People," its editors declare their confidence in the rule of law. After the horrors of 1994, when more than half a million people, including three-quarters of the Tutsi population, were murdered by Hutu extremists, it is amazing that they can have confidence in anything.

Given the United Nations' track record in the years since the genocide, Rwanda has a strong basis for its distrust.

Least of all the international community. Not only did the world abandon Rwandans to die during the slaughter, but the tribunal the United Nations set up afterwards in Arusha, Tanzania, to prosecute the most prominent *genocidaires* is now actually hindering the process of bringing them to justice.

Faulty Justice

The latest outrage is the tribunal's dithering over the fate of Jean-Bosco Barayagwiza, a founder of both a murderous Hutu Power group and the notorious anti-Tutsi radio station that helped incite the genocide. For these actions, Barayagwiza was indicted by the U.N. tribunal for genocide and crimes against humanity. When he was captured in [the west Africa country] Cameroon in March 1996 and finally shipped to Arusha in November 1997, he became one of the most notorious genocide suspects in U.N. custody. That is, until November 3, [1999] when the appeals court for the U.N. Rwanda tribunal ordered that he be set free because he had been detained at length in Cameroon without being charged and had languished in jail for too long without standing trial. Although Carla Del Ponte, the new U.N. chief prosecutor, is trying to persuade the appeals court to reconsider its decision, the Rwandan government remains furious. It has stopped cooperating with the court and is refusing even to let Del Ponte set foot in Rwanda to visit the tribunal's own prosecution office in Kigali, the nation's capital.

Given the United Nations' track record in the years since the genocide, Rwanda has a strong basis for its distrust. Having defeated the Hutu *genocidaires* after the 1994 slaughter, the new Tutsi-dominated Rwandan government wanted the international community to help catch the war criminals and then turn them over to Rwandan courts. Instead, the United Nations set up its own tribunal, which got the major suspects but—unlike at Nuremberg [, the trials for war criminals involved in the Jewish Holocaust]—did not even sit in the country it was judging. The Arusha court was also tacked on to the U.N. war crimes tribunal for the former Yugoslavia, with a single prosecutor for both tribunals and an appeals court that sits in splendid isolation in The Hague. The tribunal loftily refuses to impose the death penalty (in contrast to Rwanda), even though the Allies hanged the guilty at Nuremberg and Tokyo and Israel did the same to Adolf Eichmann, [who implemented the Nazi Final Solution aimed at totally exterminating European Jews]. And the tribunal, for years underfunded by a world that viewed its existence as a token gesture, has developed a reputation for incompetence and corruption. In 1997, an internal U.N. investigation found that "not a single administrative area functioned effectively" in the tribunal's administrative branch. The tribunal's biggest achievement has been that it has 38 high-profile suspects in custody, including former Rwandan Prime Minister Jean Kambanda, who pled guilty to genocide [in 1998]. But, if Barayagwiza walks free, even that success will be tainted.

The trials are often of the shotgun variety.

To be sure, Rwanda's own brand of justice isn't much to brag about, either. Rwanda holds some 125,000 lower-level genocide suspects in squalid and overcrowded jails, and, with its fragile judiciary system shattered by the genocide, it has only managed to try a handful of them. The trials are often of the shotgun variety. Especially outside of Kigali, defendants have been tried without counsel. In April 1998, 22 convicts were publicly shot in front of cheering crowds in public stadiums—scaring many other suspects into confessing in hopes of being granted plea bargains.

Possible Solutions

But Rwanda's internal problems are no excuse for the international tribunal's behavior. Indeed, the dallying of the latter is partially responsible for the former. Anyone at the U.N. Security Council who wants to sanction Rwanda as punishment for Del Ponte's visa problem is making a big mistake. This crisis should be an opportunity to find ways to make Rwandans take the tribunal seriously. If Barayagwiza cannot be tried in Arusha, he could still be brought before the courts of another state (Belgium has already expressed interest) under the principle of universal jurisdiction for crimes against humanity. The United Nations—and America—could give more money not just to the Arusha tribunal but also to Rwanda's courts and to efforts to train Rwandan judges. The United Nations could appoint a prosecutor for the Rwanda tribunal alone, rather than having Del Ponte handle both Rwanda and the former Yugoslavia simultaneously. And the United Nations could remember, as it often has not, that justice means more than simply following legal procedures. To endure, it must also do something for the survivors.

Important Figures in the Rwanda Genocide

Kofi Annan, undersecretary general for United Nations peacekeeping operations during the genocide; now UN secretary general.

General Maurice Baril, head of the Department of Peacekeeping Operations (DPKO) at UN Headquarters and the military adviser to UN secretary general Boutros Boutros-Ghali during the genocide. He was the recipient of the now infamous "genocide fax" sent on January 11, 1994, from General Roméo Dallaire.

General Roméo Dallaire, force commander of the United Nations Assistance Mission for Rwanda during the genocide. He sent the now infamous "genocide fax" on January 11, 1994, to General Maurice Baril in the hopes of heading off the informant-predicted genocide.

Juvenal Habyarimana, president of Rwanda. The genocide began immediately after his plane was shot down on April 6, 1994. Habyarimana and Burundian president Cyprien Ntaryamira both died in the crash.

Paul Kagame, vice president of Rwanda during the genocide. He later became president of Rwanda and in August 2003 he was voted back into office.

Cyprien Ntaryamira, president of Burundi. He was killed along with Rwandan president Juvenal Habyarimana just outside the Rwandan capital, Kigali, on April 6, 1994.

Chronology

April 6, 1994
Rwandan president Juvenal Habyarimana and Burundian president Cyprien Ntaryamira are killed when Habyarimana's plane is shot down just outside the airport in Kigali, Rwanda's capital. Hutu extremists are suspected of being behind the attack. Killings begin within hours of the crash.

April 7, 1994
The Rwandan Armed Forces (RAF) and Hutu militia (the Interhamwe) begin killing Rwandans by going from house to house. Tutsis and moderate Hutu politicians are among the first victims. Thousands of Rwandans are murdered on this first day. The majority of UN peacekeeping forces, UNAMIR (United Nations Assistance Mission in Rwanda), stationed in Rwanda stand by during the slaughter because, according to their official mandate, they are forbidden to intervene. Also on this day, ten Belgian soldiers are murdered, prompting Belgium and the UN to consider removing their troops from Rwanda.

April 8, 1994
The Rwandan Patriotic Front (RPF), a Rwandan militia, attempts to end the killings in the hopes of liberating six hundred of its own troops trapped in Kigali. U.S. president Bill Clinton issues a statement assuring the families of U.S. citizens in Rwanda that every effort is being made to secure their safety.

April 9–10, 1994
French and Belgian troops and American citizens are rescued and pulled out of Rwanda by their respective governments.

April 21, 1994
The UN Security Council votes to withdraw many of its troops. The UNAMIR force is reduced from 2,500 to 270.

May–June 1994

The press continues to ask the United States if the ongoing events in Rwanda are acts of genocide. Government officials remain unwilling to provide a clear answer to the question. Nonetheless, the killings continue. By mid-May, the International Red Cross estimates that over five hundred thousand Rwandans have been slaughtered.

May 17, 1994

The UN agrees to send fifty-five hundred troops to Rwanda. The deployment of the troops is delayed because no one can agree on who should pay the costs of such reinforcements.

May 19, 1994

The UN asks the United States to provide fifty armored personnel carriers to Rwanda. Once again, arguments ensue as to who should pay for the carriers.

June 22, 1994

The French government deploys forces in Rwanda in a military operation called Operation Turquoise. By doing so, a secured area is created.

mid-July 1994

The Rwandan Patriotic Army (RPA), the mainly Tutsi militia, finally secures Kigali, ending the genocide. The remaining Hutu government flees Rwanda along with thousands of refugees. The RPF, the governing body of the RPA, sets up a government in Kigali. During the past one hundred days, an estimated eight hundred thousand Rwandans were murdered.

For Further Research

Books

Howard Adelman and Astri Suhrke, eds., *The Path of Genocide: The Rwanda Crisis from Uganda to Zaire*. New Brunswick, NJ: Transaction, 2000.

Kathi Austin, *Rwanda/Zaire—Rearming With Impunity: International Support for the Perpetrators of the Rwandan Genocide*. New York: Human Rights Watch, 1995.

Michael N. Barnett, *Eyewitness to Genocide: The United Nations and Rwanda*. Ithaca, NY: Cornell University Press, 2002.

John A. Berry and Carol Pot Berry, eds., *Genocide in Rwanda: A Collective Memory*. Washington, DC: Howard University Press, 1999.

Boutros Boutros-Ghali, *The United Nations and Rwanda: 1993–1996*. New York: United Nations Publications, 1996.

Rosamond Carr, *Land of a Thousand Hills: My Life in Rwanda*. New York: Plume, 2000.

Alison Des Forges, *Leave None to Tell the Story: Genocide in Rwanda*. New York: Human Rights Watch, 1999.

Alain Destexhe, *Rwanda and Genocide in the Twentieth Century*. Trans. Alison Marschner. New York: New York University Press, 1995.

Philip Gourevitch, *We Wish to Inform You That Tomorrow We Will Be Killed with Our Families: Stories from Rwanda*. New York: Farrar, Straus, and Giroux, 1999.

Human Rights Watch, *Shattered Lives: Sexual Violence During the Rwandan Genocide and Its Aftermath*. New York: Human Rights Watch, 2000.

Fergal Keane, *Season of Blood: A Rwandan Journey*. New York: Viking, 1996.

Shaharyar M. Khan, *The Shallow Graves of Rwanda*. New York: I.B. Tauris, 2000.

Alan J. Kuperman, *The Limits of Humanitarian Intervention: Genocide in Rwanda.* Washington, DC: Brookings Institution, 2001.

Paul Magnarella, *Justice in Africa: Rwanda's Genocide, Its Courts, and the UN Criminal Tribunal.* Aldershot, UK: Ashgate, 2000.

Mahmood Mamdani, *When Victims Become Killers: Colonialism, Nativism, and Genocide in Rwanda.* Princeton, NJ: Princeton University Press, 2001.

Linda Melvern, *A People Betrayed: The Role of the West in Rwanda's Genocide.* New York: St. Martin's, 2000.

Elizabeth Neuffer, *The Key to My Neighbor's House: Seeking Justice in Bosnia and Rwanda.* New York: Picador, 2001.

Edward L. Nyankanzi, *Genocide: Rwanda and Burundi.* Rochester, VT: Schenkman, 1998.

Gérard Prunier, *The Rwanda Crisis: History of a Genocide.* London: C. Hurst, 1998.

Sara Rakita, *Rwanda, Lasting Wounds: Consequences of Genocide and War on Rwanda's Children.* New York: Human Rights Watch, 2003.

Richard A. Salem, ed., *Witness to Genocide, the Children of Rwanda: Drawings of Child Survivors of the Rwandan Genocide of 1994.* New York: Friendship, 2000.

Christian P. Scherrer, *Genocide and Crisis in Central Africa: Conflict Roots, Mass Violence, and Regional War.* Westport, CT: Praeger, 2002.

André Sibomana, *Hope for Rwanda: Conversations with Laure Guilbert and Hervé Deguine.* Trans. Carina Tertsakian. Sterling, VA: Pluto, 1999.

Christopher C. Taylor, *Sacrifice as Terror: The Rwandan Genocide of 1994.* New York: Berg, 1999.

Peter Uvin, *Aiding Violence: The Development Enterprise in Rwanda.* West Hartford, CT: Kumarian, 1998.

Leonard Uwiringiyimana, *The Rwanda Crisis: Genesis, Issues and Perspectives (Selected Readings).* Dayton, OH: Rwanda-Hope, 1996.

Periodicals

Pal Ahluwalia, "Specificities: The Rwandan Genocide: Exile and Nationalism Reconsidered," *Social Identities*, vol. 3, no. 3, 1997, pp. 499–519.

Douglas Anglin and Daniel C. Bach, "Confronting Rwandan Genocide. The Military Options, What Could and Should the International Community Have Done?" *Études Internationales*, vol. 34, no. 1, 2003, pp. 129–38.

Laurie Goering, "Islam Blooms in Wake of Rwandan Genocide," *Chicago Tribune*, August 8, 2002.

Christine L. Kellow and H. Leslie Steeves, "The Role of Radio in the Rwandan Genocide," *Peace Research Abstracts*, vol. 38, no. 2, 2001, pp. 38–47.

Sonja Linden, "Working with Survivors of the Rwandan Genocide," *Jewish Quarterly*, vol. 46, no. 2, 1999, pp. 5–9.

William F.S. Miles, "Hamites and Hebrews: Problems of 'Judaizing' the Rwandan Genocide," *Journal of Genocide Research*, vol. 2, no. 1, 2000, pp. 107–15.

David Newbury, "Understanding Genocide," *African Studies Review*, vol. 41, no. 1, 1998, pp. 73–97.

George S. Yacoubian Jr., "The Efficacy of International Criminal Justice: Evaluating the Aftermath of the Rwandan Genocide," *World Affairs*, vol. 161, no. 4, 1999, pp. 186–92.

Internet Sources

Amnesty International, "Rwanda." www.amnestyusa.org/country/rwanda.

Gendercide Watch, "Case Study: Genocide in Rwanda, 1984," 2000. www.gendercide.org/case_rwanda.html.

PBS, "The Triumph of Evil," *Frontline*, 1999. www.pbs.org.

Stefan Schmitt, "Statistics of a Mass Grave: The Kibuye Case," *The Rwandan Genocide*, Organization of Forensic Mission, 1998. http://garnet.acns.fsu.edu/~sss4407/Rwanda/RWStats.htm.

Stuart Stein, "Report of the Independent Inquiry into the Actions of the United Nations During the 1994 Genocide in Rwanda," Faculty of Economics and Social Science Home Page of the University of West England,

Frenchay Campus, December 15, 1999. www.ess.uwe.ac. uk/genocide/Rwanda.htm.

Emily Wax, "At the Heart of Rwanda's Horror," *Washington Post* September 21, 2002. www.washingtonpost.com.

———, "Islam Attracting Many Survivors of Rwanda Genocide," *Washington Post*, September 23, 2002. www. washingtonpost.com.

Gunnar Willum and Bjørn Willum, "The Rwanda Genocide Seen in a New Light," *Inshuti*, April 17, 2000. www2. minorisa.es/inshuti/light.htm.

Websites

International Tribunal for Rwanda, www.ictr.org. A court formed in 1995 to bring to justice the military and political leaders who deliberately manipulated the ethnic division between the Hutus and Tutsis, the tribunal's website provides links to complete transcripts of the trials that they conduct, their assessments of what went wrong in Rwanda, and the current state of affairs in that war-torn country.

Rwanda Hope Society, www.rwandahope.com. The Rwanda Hope Society, an organization established to assist the people of Rwanda by sponsoring educational and civic programs, maintains this website of background information on the Rwandan genocide and the ethnic struggle between the Hutu and Tutsis. They also include a newsletter detailing the current projects in which Rwanda Hope is involved.

Index